Misunderstood Animals

By

Alice L. Hopf

MCGRAW-HILL BOOK COMPANY

New York   St. Louis   San Francisco   Düsseldorf   Johannesburg
Kuala Lumpur   London   Mexico   Montreal   New Delhi   Panama
Rio de Janeiro   Singapore   Sydney   Toronto

Acknowledgments

Pictures appearing on pages 7, 42, 43, 51, 55, 62
Courtesy of Leonard Lee Rue III

Pictures appearing on pages 27, 38
Courtesy of Wometco Miami Seaquarium

Picture appearing on page 30
Courtesy of Treat Davidson, from National Audubon Society

Picture appearing on page 35
Courtesy of Miami Seaquarium

Pictures appearing on pages 45, 76, 78, 91
Courtesy of Bureau of Sport Fisheries & Wildlife

Pictures appearing on pages 48, 64, 83, 86, 94, 112, 119
Courtesy of San Diego Zoo

Pictures appearing on pages 67, 73
Courtesy of the U.S. Department of Agriculture

Picture appearing on page 106
Courtesy of the American Museum of Natural History

Library of Congress Cataloging in Publication Data

Hopf, Alice Lightner,
  Misunderstood animals.

  SUMMARY: Anecdotes about animals and their place in
nature.
  1. Animals, Habits and behavior of—Juvenile
literature. [1. Animals—Habits and behavior]
I. Title.
QL751.5.H66   591.5   73–6623
ISBN 0–07–030312–6

123456789 BPBP 79876543

Contents

To Teddy
who likes animals . . .
and chess . . .
and some things that are
over my head

1

They Are Only Doing Their Thing

Most persons, when they think about an animal, wonder if it is a "good animal" or a "bad animal." Is it vicious? Does it bite? What use is it?

Since the beginnings of civilization, when man first took certain animals under his care to domesticate them, through the development of farming and the building of cities, the "good" animals have tended to be the domestic animals. The cows, pigs, horses, sheep, and chickens. The majority of animals that stayed wild were looked upon as "bad." And their badness was in direct proportion to how much they interfered with man's activities.

If they were small animals, like rabbits and squirrels, that nibbled in the garden, dug up the fields, or made holes in the roof, they were dismissed as "pests," and occasional efforts were made to exterminate them. But if they were flesh eaters, like wolves or foxes, that found man's hoard of domestic meat as tasty as he did, they were marked down as cruel, vicious, slinky marauders—and it was war to the death.

5

Even today, the large predatory animals in our western states, where there would seem to be room for all, are trapped, shot from airplanes, and poisoned with a particularly insidious poison called 1080, which brings agonizing death. Not only the animals for whom it is intended die, but every animal that may later dine off a poisoned carcass also adds to a long chain of wanton killing.

There is a revealing definition of what a predator is, voiced by W. O. Nagel, a man who loved animals and the wilderness: "A predator is any creature that has beaten you to another creature you wanted for yourself." It is only recently that another idea has grown and taken hold of world opinion: that the animals that share this beautiful planet with us have as much right to life and living space as we do.

In the eighteenth century the wolves were exterminated in Scotland, at the cost of large forests put to the torch. The animals hiding in the depths of those forests had had the audacity to dine off the laird's deer. Worse than that, they had preyed on the newly introduced herds of sheep. The textile industry was beginning to develop in Britain, and wolves were not part of the plan. In addition, the poor tenant farmers were not part of the plan either. The same people who exterminated the wolves also uprooted the little farmers who had lived there for centuries, causing many of them to migrate to America. In the process, they ruthlessly burned their small villages, not caring if the old and sick were burned along with them. The ruins of these old cottages can still be seen in the Scottish hills.

Today, any such uprooting of an entire people for the benefit of a few rulers would be condemned by the whole world. But we are only just coming to the belief that animals, too, deserve their homes and habitats. In this endeavor, we in America have set aside large tracts of land as national parks, where the native animals can live, protected and undisturbed. This idea has been copied by most countries around the world. Nevertheless, with the present population explosion, there is more and more pressure being put against such parks. In Africa the land is constantly in demand for farming. Here in America we can see the struggle in places like Florida, where the Everglades National Park is threatened by developers who want to build airports and houses or to use the water supply that keeps the Everglades alive.

When people want to have something that animals (or other people) have, they can always think up good excuses. One way is to belittle the other fellow. We all know the slanders that were made up about the Indians during the "Winning of the West." If we look at the parallel situation with animals, we will see that they have been similarly slandered.

The most obvious example is the wolf, together with other members of the canine family: the fox, the coyote, the jackal, and the wild dogs of Asia and Africa. All our domestic dogs are descended from wild canines. And surely the dog, who has been called man's best friend, is the most loved and most loving of all our house pets. Some scientists even doubt that civilization could have developed without the dog. The first hoofed ani-

A wolf

mal to be domesticated is believed to have been the reindeer, and it would have been difficult for early man to control the herds of these animals without the help of the dog. Civilization developed from a hunting to a food-producing stage with the domestication of animals and plants, and the dog, man's first domestic animal, helped in the building of this new way of life.

Yet all the wild dogs are now hated and slandered by man. The lion (a cat) is referred to as king of beasts, but the wolf is considered a vicious, ferocious animal, always the villain in folklore, where we have the Big, Bad Wolf and the Wolf at the Door.

The African and Asiatic wild dogs have come in for their share of slander, being referred to as "implacable hunters" and "savage and ruthless" beasts. The smaller jackals, coyotes, and foxes are usually described as wily, sneaky, and crafty. The fox is a very ancient neighbor of ours, and a frequent character in Aesop's fables. This Greek, who wrote in the sixth century B.C., often used the fox in his stories, but seldom in a complimentary manner.

When we look more closely at these animals, we find that none of this is true. The canines are much like ourselves, being mammals and predators. They are also loving parents, clever providers, strong and adaptable creatures. They can almost all learn to love man, if treated with kindness and respect. It is only man's acquisitiveness that has made them seem to be his enemies.

These animals are not great, dangerous beasts. Certainly, none of them are as dangerous as the lion, whom we admire. In our early colonial days the "terrible, ferocious wolves" were caught in pits, where rather than waste bullets on them, a man would jump in and kill them with a club.

For many years now, Canadian naturalists and rangers have been studying the wolves in Algonquin Provincial Park in Ontario. They find the wolves to be shy and retiring animals that seldom show themselves to man.

Lois and Herbert Crisler, who made one of the early photographic studies of the wolf in Alaska, became so enchanted with the wolf pups they were studying that they brought back five to civilization and continued to study them in Colorado.

Wolves also seem to be smarter than man in one respect. They have some kind of built-in population control and never let their numbers increase beyond the food supply. So although the wolf is now protected in the park, their numbers have not increased beyond a reasonable point. And they are a boon to the prey animals, which would soon eat themselves out of grass and trees.

This has been found to be true all over the world, whether in a national park where animals are totally protected, or in wild areas where a certain amount of hunting is allowed. When all the native predators are eliminated, such as wolves, coyotes, and bears, the herd animals (deer, elk, moose, wild sheep, and goats) increase quickly. Within a few seasons they will have destroyed the good pasture by eating the grass too close to the ground. They will eat all the tree vegetation within reach and devour the new seedlings before they have a chance to grow.

When hunting is allowed to reduce the numbers of these animals, the hunters shoot the best animals, both for trophies and for food. And thus the herd deteriorates, because the least strong and healthy are left to propagate. But when the natural predators are allowed to remain in the area, they will kill only the old, the weak, and the sick among the herds, for these are the only ones they are able to catch. The strong, healthy animals are left to continue the species.

If you go to Algonquin Park in the summer, you can have the unusual experience of attending a "wolf howl." The rangers escort a group of campers in their cars to a likely spot. There the ranger will play a recording of a wolf's howl, or perhaps will howl himself. And soon the wolves will be answering, their different-toned voices building up into a thrilling chorus.

Scientists are still trying to learn why wolves howl, but of one thing they are certain—it is not a threat or a hunting cry.

It would seem to be more a social expression of love and well-being. Or possibly, it is a means of communication among separated animals. In one case, a group of wolves that seemed to be settled for the night howled and were answered by a single wolf. But instead of the lone wolf moving over to the group, the pack joined the loner! The rangers theorize that the lone wolf was the leader, and the top wolf is always held in high esteem by the rest of the pack.

Our present attitude toward the canines has not been universal. The ancient Egyptians, for instance, revered the jackal as a god. And many primitive people have a similar high regard for their canines.

Perhaps our general fear of certain animals goes back much farther than the early days of history. One eminent scientist has stated that the two creatures most feared by man are the spider and the snake. These animals differ so widely from us in their form that it is perhaps not surprising that we should feel a natural aversion. The spider has twice our number of limbs, and the snake has none at all.

Yet neither of these creatures is really dangerous, except when they harbor poison, and this is in the minority of cases. An intelligent person will learn which creatures are really poisonous and try to avoid them. For in all such instances the animal is only using its natural defenses. Snakes strike when they are stepped on or when they are attacked and cornered. And the black widow spider never goes hunting for a human to bite. It hides under stones and debris, and only when it accidentally gets into a shoe or feels itself attacked or threatened is it dangerous. Even so, the black widow is not fatal to all, for some people are more susceptible to its poison than others. And while a bite from the black widow is certainly to be avoided, more people die of bee and wasp stings than from the bite of this little spider.

Snakes and spiders both have their place in the balance of nature. A decrease in the snake population will bring a rapid increase in that of rats and mice. And spiders are extremely helpful to us in controlling the insects that would otherwise ravage our farms. The balance between these different creatures has been built up over long ages by evolution. And when we take one animal out of this intricate design, we often throw the whole out of balance, with disastrous results.

We are inclined to think that with our modern poisons and scientifically developed killing devices we can rid ourselves of the so-called bad animals. But recently we have learned how such methods can backfire. Not only do we kill off the good animals, but we are also in danger of poisoning ourselves.

So let us forget the old wives' tales and the ancient folklore that pin tags of good or bad on all the world's creatures. Let us try to realize that these animals, many of them so different from us, but many so like us, are only doing their thing. They are living as nature intended them to live. Each one has its place in the evolutionary scheme, a place that was worked out in the struggle for survival over long eons of time. And each has as much right as we have to enjoy its span of life on this planet.

2

The Killer Whale
(Orcinus orca)

Perhaps the worst case of our misunderstanding of an animal is
that of the killer whale. Until 1964 this great beast was considered one of the most vicious, ferocious, and deadly in the
world. But since it is a creature of the wide oceans, it is seldom
seen by the average citizen. Thus, most descriptions and reports
of the killer whale have come from sailors, whalers, and coastal
fishermen.

The orcas belong to the order of sea-dwelling mammals
(Cetacea) that includes the whales, dolphins, and porpoises. The
orca is bigger than some whales, such as the dolphins, and
smaller than the larger whales. It is a striking animal, with con-
trasting color patches of black and white. The male grows to
a length of thirty feet, but the female is smaller. The dorsal
fin rises six feet from its back and is used to stabilize the animal
in the water.

These huge beasts, weighing up to nine tons, are among the
most powerful animals in existence and are found in all the

Two killer whales

oceans from the Arctic to the Antarctic. They can propel themselves through the water at a top speed of 23 miles an hour and can overtake any creature that swims. Sea lions, penguins, and other whales all get out of the way fast when a killer whale approaches.

One report tells of a killer whale that seized a 600-pound sea lion in its jaws and flung it several times into the air, playing with it as a cat does with a mouse, before finally eating it. The killer is well supplied with teeth for such activities. Fifty big conical teeth are set in his huge jaw so that they interlock. They are used for tearing rather than chewing. The prey is often swallowed whole.

Orcas have been called the wolves of the sea, and like the wolves, they are social animals. They travel in packs (or pods) of from a few individuals up to several dozen or even more. A herd numbering in the hundreds probably represents a migration rather than a hunting group. It is likely that they may have a social life resembling that of the wolves, but scientist-skin divers are only now beginning to study this social life.

Reports of whalers tell of packs of these animals pursuing and killing the largest animal in the world—the great blue whale. Since the whalers were also hunting the whale, it was the old story of whose right to kill took precedence, and the seamen were quick to brand orcas as bloodthirsty killers. They describe how the smaller beasts would leap out of the water and come down on the great whale's back, thrashing and worrying it, while others of the pack rushed in to tear out its tongue. When the wounded whale finally bled to death, the pack of killers feasted.

The great blue whale is an inoffensive beast. It has no teeth with which to fight its enemies. Instead, its mouth is full of whalebone strainers. It opens its huge maw and takes a mouthful of water. When the water strains out, the tiny plankton are caught behind the strainers and swallowed. The largest animal in the ocean feeds on one of the smallest forms of life! However, it is believed that sometimes these placid animals become provoked by the attacking orcas and can beat them off with a flip of their

giant tail fins. How many of these blue-whale hunts are successful for the orcas can only be guessed at. We know that the wolf
pack succeeds in killing only the old and the sick among the
moose and caribou. Perhaps this is true in the ocean as well.

In her book *There's a Seal in My Sleeping Bag,* Lyn Han-
cock tells of a killer whale hunt observed by her husband along
the coast of British Columbia. A minke whale, a medium-sized
whale, had been chased into a shallow bay by a group of killer
whales. There were seven whales in the attacking pack, three
adult males, two adult females, and two calves. The males did
the attacking, while the females and their calves stayed on the
outskirts of the action and waited until the minke whale was
dead. When the larger animal had bled to death and sunk to
the bottom, all the orcas dived down after it, coming up re-
peatedly with choice pieces of meat, which they ate sometimes
above and sometimes below the surface.

While killer whales will eat fish, they seem to prefer warm-
blooded animals, and they pursue seals, dolphins, and even
penguins relentlessly. Only the full-grown walrus, with its big
tusks, is able to defeat a pod of orcas. Even when the hunted
animals retreat onto the ice, they are not safe. Killers are adept
at judging where the victim is on the ice floe, and will swim
underwater and hit the ice a mighty blow, sometimes tipping it
up so that the prey falls into the sea, or splitting the floe into
smaller pieces so that the fleeing animal cannot escape.

This strategy of the killer whales was vividly described by
a photographer who went to the Antarctic with Robert F. Scott's
expedition in 1911. Herbert G. Ponting was standing on the ice
near a group of sled dogs, which were tied to stakes. When he
saw a pack of killer whales approaching, he got out his camera
and prepared to take a picture. The killers disappeared in the
water, and Ponting began to focus his camera, when he realized
that the ice was breaking up under his feet! He was forced to
jump from one cake of ice to another to reach the safety of the
shore.

"As I looked back," he wrote, "a huge black and tawny

head was pushed out of the water at the spot, and rested on the ice, looking round with its little pig-like eyes to see what had become of me. The brute opened his jaw wide, and I saw the terrible teeth which I had so narrowly escaped."

Later writers have surmised that the killers may have been hunting the dogs, which must have resembled sleeping seals to the whales. Fortunately, the chains held and the dogs were not thrown into the sea.

Another famous story of killer-whale aggressiveness comes from California as recently as 1952. Two men were fishing in a small boat when a huge "deep-sea monster" approached. They rowed frantically for shore, but the creature, after circling the boat, charged them and sank its teeth into the wood. One of the men beat off their attacker with an oar, and they reached shore just as their boat began to sink.

Although the men insisted that they had been attacked by a killer whale, they described the beast as dark brown. When the chewed-up boat was examined later by Victor B. Scheffer, a noted authority on sea animals, it was determined that the villain in this case was not a killer whale but a great white shark. Sharks and whales have very different teeth, and the evidence of the teeth marks in the boat was conclusive.

Unlike many sea monsters that have been feared from ancient days, there is little written about the killer whale in early histories. The stories of its ferocious behavior all come from whaling days or from the first white sailors who explored the Pacific and Antarctic oceans. The Eskimos hunted the polar seas for untold generations, with nothing bigger than their little kayaks as protection. But there are no stories of attacks by this animal. Like all primitive peoples, the Eskimos recognize the strength and daring of a powerful predator, but they do not condemn it as dangerous and criminal. The Indians of our Northwest referred to the orcas as people—powerful people living in the sea.

One other legend about the killer whale should have prepared us for recent events. This is a story of its cooperation with man! Every year, with the changing seasons, the larger whales swim great distances, from north to south or vice versa, much as the birds migrate through the sky. One such migration went past Twofold Bay in southeastern Australia. Early in the nineteenth century white settlers began to catch these whales. Then they discovered that a pack of killer whales would arrive just before the migration and wait for the big whales to put in an appearance. When the humpbacks and the right whales swam past on their way north, the killers would rush out and attack them, leaping and splashing excitedly. They herded the whales into the bay, much as a wolf pack herds caribou. There the whalers harpooned them and dragged them to shore. But they always rewarded the killers with a goodly portion of the whale's anatomy. This encouraged the pack to turn up the next year and repeat their little herding job.

This remarkable cooperation between man and beast has been on the records since the beginning of the last century, but few people paid any attention to it. They preferred to believe the stories of the bloodthirsty nature of the killer whale. It gave them an excuse for shooting the orcas with high-powered rifles.

And then the first killer whales were captured alive in the 1960's—and the whole picture changed. In 1961 a specimen was caught off southern California. But it was a sick animal and died two days later. Then, in 1964, an orca was harpooned by collectors for the Vancouver Public Aquarium. They had expected to get a dead whale, but when they found the animal was only stunned, they decided to tow it the forty miles to Vancouver. There it was kept in a pen for eighty-seven days, during which time it became famous. Thousands of people came to see it. A contest by radio picked its name: Moby Doll. For it was believed to be a female. Later, when it died, it was found to be a male. But during his short life in captivity, he starred in a movie and his voice was heard by millions of people over the radio. Scientists hastened to study this first captive *Orcinus orca*. But eighty-seven days is not a very long time in which to observe such a remarkable animal, and there was great disappointment when Moby Doll died.

Six months later, another killer whale was accidentally caught in the nets of some fishermen. The place was near the village of Namu in British Columbia, so this whale became known as Namu. The fishermen fenced him in behind nets while they looked for a buyer. Edward Griffin, director of the Seattle Aquarium, bought him for eight thousand dollars, and then constructed a special floating tank in which to tow him the 450 miles to Seattle.

During the early part of the trip, the group was followed by a pack of killer whales that swam around the boats and tried to charge the tank. They were warned off by their sonar, and would stop just short of hitting it. After the main pack departed, a female and two calves continued with the convoy for 150 miles, and observers believed they were part of Namu's own family. All the time that these whales were near the tank, they could be heard "talking" to Namu with their strange screams, squeaks, and whistles.

Installed in a large tank on the Seattle waterfront, Namu quickly became famous. In the *National Geographic* for March 1966, Griffin tells how he won the trust and friendship of this great sea beast. Namu was twenty-four feet long and weighed five tons, and he ate 400 pounds of fish a day. He soon learned to take the fish from Griffin's hand and allowed himself to be patted and scratched. And then Griffin took the big step. He got into the tank with Namu!

There is little doubt that the watchers expected to see Griffin chewed up, if not swallowed whole. But this remarkable and understanding man felt that he could trust his animal. He tells how he offered the whale a salmon, while crouching on the dock at the end of the tank. Namu took the fish in his jaws, but this time Griffin did not let go of his end. He held on and was dragged into the water for a distance of thirty feet. He then released his hold on the fish and Namu swallowed it. Griffin started to swim back to the dock, but to his amazement, the whale came up under him and carried him swiftly to his destination. Namu wanted another fish!

Namu had a mind of his own. Griffin tells of one day when the whale kept begging for fish. Each time he was offered a salmon, he grabbed it and quickly sank below the surface. Then he was back in record time, begging for another. At last, Griffin decided to find out what was going on. He jumped in and dove to the bottom of the tank, where he found that Namu had stacked the fish in a neat little pile, like so much cordwood. Apparently, he was hoarding his rations to eat between feedings!

These and other incidents have convinced observers that killer whales have a very high intelligence. They seem to communicate with each other in much the same way that dolphins do, and they have the same sonar system, typical of all whales and porpoises, by which they find their way in the dark depths of the ocean. This echo system (similar to that used by bats) gives so high a sound that the human ear cannot hear it, and is so exact that the animal can tell not only the size and shape of objects at a distance but also the *kind* of fish!

The great undersea explorer Jacques Cousteau says quite positively that the killer whale is more intelligent than the dolphin and learns faster. He and his colleagues have chased these animals through the sea in their speedboat, called the *Zodiac*. He tells how the killers, when they find they cannot outrun this high-speed machine, will resort to all kinds of tricks to get away. In one case, the big male made a great commotion in the water and led the boat away, while the rest of the pod escaped in the opposite direction. When sufficient distance had been achieved, the big leader quickly dove into the depths and did not surface until he popped up in the middle of his distant pack.

Cousteau and his divers also visited captive orcas and found them very receptive to guitar music. They came to the side of their tank to listen and applauded by spraying the guitarist with water.

It is believed that the whales and dolphins were once land animals, but that millions of years in the past they returned to the sea, from which all life has evolved. In going back to the sea, their front legs developed into fins, and the remains of the ancient leg bones are still there. The hind legs have completely disappeared and become the paired tail fins, or flukes. This change happened so many millions of years ago that the animals can no longer live on land. The seals and sea lions make up another group of animals that may be returning to the sea, but they have been living in the water a much shorter period of time and have not changed their form to such an extent. They must go back to the land to mate and bear their young.

A killer whale surfacing

The killer whale mates and gives birth in the ocean, and it has developed special methods of doing this. The baby is always born tail first. If it were born head first—as is usual with most land animals—the baby would drown before it could get out of the mother and rise to the surface for air. As soon as it is born, the mother pushes it to the surface for its first breath of air.

Another adjustment the whales have made is in nursing the babies. The mother whale has two apertures near her tail, and when the baby (a baby killer whale is seven feet long) nuzzles her, she shoots milk from the aperture into its mouth. Observers at Marineland, Florida, watching the birth of a dolphin, reported that the newborn baby nuzzled the mother all over before finding the right spot! This search went on every time the baby fed, until it finally learned and remembered the right place.

Namu became an object of great interest to scientists from all over. They came to study the whale's sonar and "language." They listened to his heartbeat and took samples of his blood. They investigated his unusual system of breathing. Whales and dolphins have their nasal openings on the top of the head, instead of in front, as with most animals. They can spout water through this hole, and there is a flap that closes when the animal dives.

Namu was given every medical attention that science could devise, including vitamin shots, which were pumped into him with a bow and arrow and which seemed not to bother the great beast at all. In spite of all this care, Namu died in the summer of 1966. It was a great blow to Griffin and all the whale's friends in the Pacific Northwest. Namu had shown plainly that he wanted to be loved. He wanted to have his head patted and his stomach rubbed. He enjoyed playing games with his trainer. One time, when Griffin was swimming with him, he accidentally got one leg in the whale's mouth. The great beast could easily have bitten it off. But he rolled in such a way that the man's leg slipped out without a scratch from the sharp teeth.

Cousteau is convinced that in spite of their great strength and frightening array of teeth, the orcas are not aggressive toward man and have never attacked divers. Many animals that have been chased unrelentingly, as Cousteau pursued the killer whales with his speedboat, would have turned and attacked their pursuers. The killer whales never did so, although they could easily have destroyed the frail little craft.

Since then, a number of killer whales have been captured and are being exhibited and studied at aquariums around the world. One of the most famous is Shamu, a female at Sea World in San Diego. And there is Hugo at the Seaquarium near Miami, and his consort, Lolita, who can jump twenty feet out of the water, coming down with a splash that drenches the audience. There may be as many as forty killers now in captivity, and their price has risen to $20,000 for one whale. Many of them are trained to perform, and often this performance includes giving the man a friendly kiss with the whale's tongue or allowing him to put his head inside the great jaws!

This catching of orcas has made scientists and naturalists worry about their future. The larger whales are all in danger of extinction because of relentless killing by whalers. Until now, there has been no commercial value placed on the killer whale. But with the recent astronomical prices being paid for captured orcas, they are being hunted for zoos and research. Many are killed in the process, and if they do not have proper care, they die in captivity. For this reason, the state of Washington, in whose waters much of the catching goes on, has begun to control the business. In 1971 a law was passed setting up an expensive licensing system. It is administered by the State Game and Fish Department. Even if a catcher managed to trap a whale outside state waters, he would not be able to bring it ashore in Washington without complying with this law.

Science is beginning to find uses for the new knowledge about these whales. The recordings made of their screams and whistles have been used to frighten away other sea animals. In one operation, it is hoped that it may chase porpoises out of the big nets used to catch tuna. The porpoises often swim with the tuna and are caught when the nets are pulled in. Almost a million porpoises have been unnecessarily killed in this manner. Perhaps when they hear the dreaded cries of the killer whales, they will jump out of the nets and so save themselves.

Such an experiment has already been successful in Alaska, where a great salmon run takes place every spring. The young salmon going out to sea are preyed upon by herds of white whales, which go up the river ten or twenty miles to feed on them. To protect the young salmon, the recorded cries of killer whales were broadcast underwater, and the white whales at once turned tail and fled against the tide!

So this is the fearsome, ravening beast about which so many scare stories have been told. If a captive whale can so quickly learn to love its captor, it is probable that in the wild this love is directed toward the other members of the pack.

And this is, indeed, what students of these whales have found. Cousteau states that the killer whale family is a closely united group. Having only one calf at a time, the mother surrounds it with love and attention. She talks to it in their language of clicks and squeaks. In one case, a dying female swam round and round her baby, trying to protect it until her strength was gone. And in another case, when a baby whale was killed in Puget Sound, the mother swam up and down for three days before she would leave the spot where her calf had been killed.

Cousteau says that killer whales have very soft skins and often swim closely together, rubbing against each other affectionately. He says that in captivity they can easily tell the difference between men and women. And he tells of the experience of one whale-keeper who was pinned against the tank wall by a female orca while she affectionately rubbed against him. No amount of herring, thrown into the opposite end of the tank, could lure her away. The diver had to put up with her demonstrations of affection for an hour and a half!

The groups of wild killers that followed the captive Namu as he was towed on the long trek to Seattle seem to bear this out. They squeaked and whistled to him and he replied. This behavior reminds us of that of wolves and foxes, which stay near their trapped mates, often refusing to leave, so that they also are killed by the hunter. Any animal that exhibits such devotion to its kind can hardly be listed as a bloodthirsty monster.

A number of scientists are trying to decipher the language of killer whales. Because these animals are even more intelligent than the brilliant dolphin, it is hoped that it may be possible to bridge the language gap with them. But to date, no such breakthrough has been achieved. However, Cousteau believes this is a great challenge and that possibly in the future we may be able to establish communication with these extraordinary animals of the sea.

3

The Octopus
(*Octopus vulgaris*)

The octopus has been looked upon with fear and loathing since the very earliest times, possibly because an animal with eight arms or legs must always appear to be a monstrous creature to a human biped. Greek mythology is full of deadly monsters with snakes instead of hair that could kill with a glance. These legends were probably inspired by the octopus, as was the story in Homer's *Odyssey* of Ulysses' battle with Scylla. This monster lived in a cavern under a cliff, whence she reached out with her many long necks and grabbed sailors off their ships. The description can only refer to a giant octopus.

Since the average person rarely comes in contact with an octopus, and since most people love a horror story, these legends have grown with little reference to the truth. Even such famous writers as Jules Verne and Victor Hugo have used the animal to supply dramatic and scary scenes in their novels. In Verne's *Twenty Thousand Leagues Under the Sea,* the attacking monsters were giant squids, a related species. Although squids seem to be more aggressive toward man than octopuses are, the description of their behavior is still a long way from reality.

The ship of Ulysses between Scylla and Charybdis

In truth, the octopus is a shy and retiring creature, hiding among the rocks and fleeing at the first hint of danger. There are some 150 species of octopuses, ranging in size from two inches across to giants of thirty-five feet. These last make up most of that length with their arm spread, the head and body being only about two feet in diameter. They are a very ancient form of life, with fossils as old as 400 million years.

If you can forget your first dislike of an animal that is built entirely differently from yourself, you will find that the octopus is one of the most extraordinary and fascinating creatures that has developed on this planet. To begin with, it is related to the oyster. It is a kind of advanced shellfish that has outgrown its shell and developed the ability to move around.

The octopus is an invertebrate. This means that it has no backbone or skeleton. The head and body are connected without a neck, and the eight arms are attached to the head. For this reason, scientists have put the octopus and its relatives in a group called cephalopods, meaning head-footed.

The octopus moves by jet propulsion, something that man has only developed in recent years. A siphon, or funnel, projects from its body, and by shooting water from the siphon, the octopus can move quickly in the opposite direction. But it has many other ways of moving. Sometimes it reaches out its arms and clamps its suckers to a rock. Then it pulls itself across the space between. Or it can tiptoe across a sandy bottom, using its arms like legs. Or it can float down through the water with its arms spread and the web connecting them acting like a parachute. Each arm of the octopus has one or two rows of round suckers on the underside. The number of suckers varies with the species. The common octopus has 240 suckers on each arm, making a total of 1,920. With these the animal can anchor itself securely to a rock or grab hold of a crab or other quarry and pull it into its lair. There it carves up its meal with its sharp, parrotlike beak. The octopus eye is large and round, and is remarkably like the human eye in construction.

An octopus

These are only a few of the amazing things about the octopus. There seems to be no limit to its unusual abilities. It can change color with a speed and range unknown in other creatures. Even inside the egg, the baby octopus can be seen changing color. When they are angry or excited, these creatures become red. When they are frightened, they fade to white. They can also turn blue or green or any shape in between. They can even produce a striped or mottled effect to match the spot where they are sitting.

It is no wonder that the octopus is shy and retiring, when we consider how many animals, including man, find it good eating. Fish, eels, porpoises, seals, and many other ocean creatures are given to eating octopuses, and until these animals reach a large size, they are heavily preyed upon. Even the aggressive giant squids are the prey of the great sperm whales, and sailors have reported seeing these monsters in a battle to the death. Captured whales often have the sucker marks of such squids branded into their flesh, giving a vivid picture of the struggle that took place before the victim succumbed.

The chief enemy of the common octopus is the moray eel, and the octopus has many ways of escaping from it. One is to eject a cloud of ink from its siphon. This momentarily blinds the eel and gives the octopus a chance to flee. But the clever mollusk does not only throw out a smoke screen. The cloud of ink is often shaped and colored like an octopus. At the same time, the creature changes color and darts off in the opposite direction. So while the eel is chasing a shadow octopus, the real animal, now almost white, is hiding under some rock.

But should the moray somehow smell out its quarry and get a hold on one of its arms, the octopus can still get away. It allows the arm to break off, and escapes, leaving a small piece if itself with its pursuer. Later, it hides in its cave and grows a new arm. Some scientists believe it is even capable of growing a new eye.

The octopus is also a great escape artist. It can get out of almost any cage or pot that offers only the smallest opening. For this reason, octopuses present a problem in captivity. Many an aquarium tender has gone to bed thinking his octopuses were safely confined, only to find the tank empty in the morning! Often the animals will turn up in another tank, making a meal of the occupant. Since the octopus has no bones (the only hard substance that must get through the hole is its beak), it can squeeze and flatten its arms and even its whole body. Thus, it seems to seep or ooze through the smallest crack or hole.

Octopuses live in all the oceans of the world and as deep as a mile down. They are found in the Arctic and the Antarctic, as well as at the equator. They are solitary animals, and each one needs a hole or cranny among the rocks in which to hide from its enemies. In some parts of the ocean, where there are few rocks, the octopuses fight each other for the few homes available, and the loser must move away. While they are looking for another safe place, they are very vulnerable to attack by eels or sharks. Fishermen who are out to catch octopuses know this. They lower a jar into the water with a long rope attached. After a while, the jar is pulled up, and there is a good chance that it will have an octopus in it. The unfortunate animal had been looking for a safe retreat!

Mating among octopuses is as strange as their other life habits. In the male, one arm grows into what the scientists call a hectocotylus. This carries the sperm, and the male inserts this arm inside the female's mantle—the large bag of skin that envelops the head and body. In different species, different arms are used for this purpose. In the common octopus, it is the third right arm. Once the female has received the sperm, her eggs become fertilized as they develop.

The female then retreats to her own private cave and lays her eggs. If she cannot find a suitable cave, she builds one by piling up stones and other debris around some rocky crevice. Her eggs are laid in long ribbons that are attached to the roof or sides of the cave. A mature female of the common octopus may lay up to 50,000 eggs.

The mother octopus takes good care of her eggs. She seldom

leaves her cave and often stops eating entirely. She shoots water over the eggs to keep them clean of fungus, and she rushes out to attack any threatening creature that approaches. It takes about fifty days for the eggs to hatch. After that, the baby octopuses are on their own. Some live for a time at the surface of the sea, among the plankton, where they can find food. Other species take up their life on the bottom as soon as they hatch. They no longer have the help and protection of their mother, who often dies after her brood has hatched. Only a fraction live to grow big. The rest provide food for larger animals and fish.

Within the past few decades, when men have been exploring the underwater world of the oceans and new diving equipment is constantly being invented, it has become possible to study animals like the octopus in their natural habitat. Jacques Cousteau developed a camera on the end of a long rod, which he inserted into the den of a brooding octopus in order to photograph her eggs. His divers followed her around on the ocean floor, observing and noting just how she lived. This investigator,

An octopus

as well as others, has given intelligence tests to octopuses. They have found that the creature has a high IQ for a mollusk.

In one interesting test, a live lobster was placed in a glass jar. There was a cork stopper in the mouth of the jar and a small hole had been drilled in the cork. The jar was taken to sea, and one of Cousteau's divers took it down and put it in front of the entrance to the home of an octopus. Octopuses are very fond of lobsters, so in spite of the fact that it was surrounded by cameras and lights and interested divers, the octopus came out and threw itself upon the lobster. It quickly found that while it could see its prey, it could not reach it. It turned red with anger and surprise, for the octopus displays its emotions by changing color.

The octopus first used its natural means of subduing a lobster. It wrapped its arms around the jar and covered it with its mantle. Normally, the poison from its salivary glands would have paralyzed its victim. But it could see the lobster moving around inside the jar. It became very impatient, and after a while, when the usual methods did not work, the octopus began to explore the bottle. It then found the stopper, and soon one of its arms discovered the hole in the cork and squeezed inside. When the tip of the arm touched the lobster and the lobster moved, the octopus seemed electrified. It changed color continually and set to feeling all over the stopper. It seemed to realize that the stopper could be moved, and in a few minutes it had pulled it out of the jar with one arm and two other arms were inside, collecting the lobster.

In laboratory tests, an octopus has been offered a crab on a small white plate that was electrically charged. Each time the octopus touched the crab, it received an electric shock. It quickly learned to refuse food that was offered on the white plate and to eat only if that object was not in view.

The development of scuba diving has brought problems to the swimmer as well as to the octopus. There is no doubt that if a fairly large octopus should seize hold of an inexperienced diver, and at the same time was firmly anchored by its other arms to a rock or other solid object, it might hold the diver down until he drowned. An octopus has great strength and holding power for its size. But an experienced swimmer, with modern diving equipment, should have no trouble in getting free.

The greatest threat presented by one of these creatures is from a small (six inches long) blue octopus that lives in Australian waters. Until recent years, this species was thought to be very rare and was hardly ever seen. But with the great increase in scuba diving, and with swimmers constantly exploring the Australian reefs, it has been found that this octopus poses a serious threat. The first recorded death from octopus poison came from Darwin, Australia, in 1954. Two swimmers were wading ashore when one of them noticed a little blue octopus and picked it up. In a playful mood, he threw it to his companion, who let it crawl across his shoulders before it dropped off into the surf. That unfortunate young man had barely reached the shore when he collapsed with violent pains and shortness of breath. Help was summoned, but the swimmer was dead by the time he reached a hospital. At first there was some doubt as to whether it was the bite of the octopus that had killed him. But since then there have been other victims, and scientists are now working on an antidote. The poison of this particular octopus (*Octopus maculosus*) is said to be extremely venomous.

Most octopuses secrete a toxin that they use to subdue their prey. They do not have fangs to inject it, as do the snakes, but they manage to get it into their victims. However, most octopus venom is quite harmless to people and no more noticeable than a bee sting. In fact, an octopus has far more to fear from a man than vice versa. However, they are said to be very curious, and divers report that they may become quite friendly if they are not frightened. One diver tells of an octopus that would come out and sit on his hand or foot if he remained quiet. He says he was never bitten.

Today, scientists use scuba-diving techniques to study the

octopus where it lives, in the ocean. Sometimes there is a program of tagging, and even large animals are pulled from their holes and marked for scientific study.

Dr. Gilbert L. Voss of the University of Miami, writing in the *National Geographic,* tells of diving off the Florida Keys, where his students discovered a female octopus guarding a clutch of eggs. Dr. Voss wanted the eggs for scientific study, but when he reached out for them, the mother reared up and threatened him. All the time, her body changed color in typical octopus fashion. Dr. Voss did not want to challenge her with his bare hands. He had a small metal rod with which he poked the octopus, hoping to pry loose the eggs. When the metal bar touched the mother octopus, she pulled back. She seemed to be thinking over the problem. Then, to his amazement, she began to brush the eggs with her arms and to break them open. Squirting a cloud of ink, the baby octopuses shot out and disappeared into the turtle grass. When they were all gone, the mother followed, and Dr. Voss was left with 120 egg capsules, only three of which still held baby octopuses.

Dr. Voss also tells of an unusual behavior pattern that he has noted in his observation of this animal. By microscopic study, he has found that baby octopuses sometimes hold tiny sections of the poisonous tentacles from the Portuguese man-of-war. These deadly strings of stinging tentacles, cut to the proper size, are held in place by the octopus' suckers. Whether they are used for defense or for killing prey is unknown. But it would seem to represent the use of a tool by this remarkable invertebrate.

These are only two examples of the new facts being discovered about the octopus. Do they spring from instinct, or do they show a kind of intelligence? With more work and study, Dr. Voss hopes to find out.

4

The Manta Ray
(Manta birostris)

Any animal that grows to a great size is bound to seem a threat
to the people who come in contact with it. Without having investigated the habits or intentions of the animal, men are apt to
run first and talk afterward. And in order to account for their
precipitous retreat, they tell tall tales, designed to build up the
menace of the beast that has frightened them.

This has been the history of the manta ray, often called the
devilfish or giant devil ray. Little is actually known about these
monsters of the sea. Rays are a peculiar kind of fish that lie flat
in the water instead of standing vertically. They use their two
lateral fins to fly through the water in much the same way that
birds use their wings in the air.

Every sea diver or fisherman is acquainted with the smaller
stingray, which lies hidden in the sand and can give an unwary
wader a painful sting with its poisonous tail. The manta ray is a
much larger relative without the poisonous sting. In fact, its only

defense—or offense—is its extraordinary size. These fish can grow to measure twenty feet or more across the fins and to weigh over 3,000 pounds! But like the largest of the whales (the blue whale), they eat only small ocean organisms: plankton, shrimp, and small fish. They could hardly put up much of a fight, as they are poorly supplied with teeth. Of the three related genera of devil rays, one has teeth in both jaws; the second has teeth only in the upper jaw; and the third, the manta, has teeth only in the lower jaw. They capture their prey by swimming with their great jaws agape. The weird lobes (called cephalic fins) that protrude from each side of the head flap open and shut, thus carrying the food into the mouth.

A manta ray

Mantas are colored in varying shades of black and brown and have a long, thin tail. But it is the "cephalic horns," peculiar to the devil fish, that have given it its name. When it is seen flitting through the water, its batlike form and protruding horns bring to mind all the fearful superstitions of the ignorant. And its immense size and great strength serve to enhance this view. Yet basically, this is a gentle creature, feeding on the smallest prey. It has never been known to attack man aggressively. If in its headlong flight it should hit a swimmer or overturn a boat, it would do so quite unintentionally.

Mantas are feared by fishermen, who claim that they occasionally rub against the anchor chains of their boats. This causes the boats to drift dangerously, and sometimes the chains get tangled around the monster's head and it flees in a panic, dragging the boat with it. This makes for a hazardous situation for all in the boat, and explains why fishermen have always called this fish the devil ray. However, scientists believe that the creature is merely trying to scratch itself on the anchor chain, much as a bear scratches against a tree. It seems that mantas are plagued by parasites, especially on the inner surfaces of those "horns." When a manta comes upon an anchor chain, it makes use of it to rid itself of these bothersome pests, thus causing all the confusion at the upper end of the chain.

Harold W. McCormick and Tom Allen, in their book *Shadows in the Sea,* state that the manta's horny lobes are very sensitive to anything they touch and close instantly around approaching prey. In this manner, they say, a whole school of mantas once got themselves stuck to the posts of a fence that ran out into shallow water. They go on to explain that these cephalic fins are quite weak and that there is no record of any swimmer ever having been seized by them. But the fish itself is so big and powerful that it could easily upset a boat when thrashing around after being harpooned.

Mantas are found around the world in tropic and subtropical waters. They are also seen in the Western Hemisphere from

Brazil to the Carolinas and on our West Coast as far north as Redondo Beach. This great fish has left the sandy sea bottoms, frequented by the smaller rays, to hunt in the surface waters, where plankton life abounds. The manta has its great, square mouth at the end of its head, instead of underneath as with other species. And it takes in water for breathing through the mouth instead of through its spiracles, as other fish do. It is a very powerful beast, often leaping five feet or more into the air, and it has been known to tow a twenty-five-foot motorboat for ten miles.

Perhaps it is no wonder that it has been feared by fishermen since ancient times and has been called the most vicious and evil animal in the sea. However, in recent times, since adventurous swimmers have taken to snorkel and scuba diving and to exploring and photographing the underwater world, many of these myths have been exploded.

Hans Hass, a German swimmer and photographer, found it was possible to swim among a school of mantas with impunity. He writes of his experiences while studying them in his book *Manta*. He describes the great joy of living expressed by these graceful animals as they flapped their great flippers, swam in a tight little circle, or leaped exuberantly out of the sea, to come down in crashing spray.

When a manta caught sight of the swimming photographer, its reaction was uneasy fear or curiosity. On several occasions Hass swam among a shoal of as many as forty mantas and learned to distinguish individuals by their color or by special markings. One had a kind of tumorous growth in its head. And another, which became especially useful to him, was deformed in that it had only one "horn." This made it possible for him to photograph the giant's mouth, where he had observed some little striped pilot fish. In the normal mantas, the horns got in the way. And when he tried to approach from the front, the fish were frightened and retreated inside the monster's mouth. The manta itself also became nervous and dashed away. But with the one-

A manta ray with sucker fish

horned manta, Hass could approach from the side and get a good picture. He saw that these giants have little fish that swim about inside their jaws, and he believes that they clean the mantas' mouths of parasites, and by doing so, earn themselves a safe haven.

He also observed that each manta had a suckerfish swimming underneath it, following its every move. As he swam among the mantas, photographing the suckerfish and the pilot fish, he noticed two individual mantas, which he recognized by their markings. They seemed also to recognize him after the third or fourth meeting. And he reasons that mantas probably have a fairly high IQ, as he had never seen this reaction among ordinary, smaller fish.

Hass felt that his only danger was the possibility of being inadvertently run down by one of the huge beasts. These gatherings seemed to be for mating purposes, as well as for feeding, and he says that a pair would seem to go mad and tear through the sea in a furious chase, running down anything in their way.

On several occasions he threw himself to one side only just in time, and he developed a method of rolling up in a ball with his head in the middle, to escape injury.

In mating, the female manta turns over on her back and the male swims above her. Mantas produce living young and, as far as is known, only one at a birth. There are reports of the harpooning of female mantas, which then leaped high in the air and violently ejected their offspring. Whether this was from fright and pain or as a desperate effort to save the baby is not known. Some scientists believe that mantas leap out of the sea in the process of giving birth. The underwater photographer Roberto Fabbri, writing in *Sea Frontiers,* saw a manta leap from the sea and prepared to photograph it when it came down. To his surprise, he found that he had captured the moment of birth. The baby manta (called a pup) appeared with its fins folded in a neat package. As it gradually unfolded into a miniature of its huge parent, the mother hovered over it for a few moments. Then she shot off into the ocean depths, leaving the youngster to fend for itself. The baby manta drifted slowly downward until it settled on a reef. Apparently, the pups are born with everything they need to start life alone. Alone it would have to learn to swim, to find food, to survive. But even at this earliest stage, the manta has some protection in its size. For a baby manta is usually four feet across and can weigh as much as twenty pounds.

5

The Snapping Turtle
(Chelydra serpentina)

Turtles are one of the very old forms of life on this planet. Their defensive shell evolved some 200 million years ago. And while some other reptiles developed great size or the power of flight and finally became extinct, the turtle remained much the same, lugging its house and fortress along with it down through the ages. Today these primitive animals are still with us, while their cousins, the dinosaurs, have vanished from the earth.

A number of years ago there used to be turtles in the creek near our house. Around sunset, it was our practice to stand on the bridge and throw bread crumbs to the fish, and often a number of turtles turned up to compete with the fish for this bounty. The turtles added considerably to the show, for we were soon able to identify individuals. One might be very shy, and another active and daring, and so on.

But the most interesting turtle always appeared in one corner near the bridge. It was a medium-sized snapping turtle, and when it raised its long neck and heavy head out of the weeds, we felt that we were seeing something from a different age. We threw out more bread for it to snap up and counted it a lucky day when we saw the snapper.

Each summer this turtle returned to the creek, but we were careful not to tell our neighbors about it. We realized that snappers have a price on their heads for several reasons: they are considered good eating by gourmets, and they are anathema to those who cherish fish and ducks.

Nevertheless, our silence was not enough to protect our snapper. Some years after it first appeared near the bridge, it was killed by two neighbor boys. Apparently, there was no reason for their act except that the snapper has a bad name. This one was pulled from the water, and when a stick was thrust at it and it grabbed hold with its beak, its neck was pulled out and the head chopped off. As far is I know, they did not even make money by selling it for food. For them, it was a good deed in ridding the earth of a varmint.

The snapping turtle has the widest range of any turtle in America. It is found from southern Canada to Florida and from the Atlantic states to the Rockies. It lives almost entirely in the water. If you should find a snapper wandering in the fields, it is pretty sure to be a female, looking for a place to lay her eggs. These turtles are not particular about the kind of water they live in, and are found in running streams as well as in placid ponds. They can live even in salt marshes, and one specimen was caught swimming in Buzzards Bay. But the snapper especially likes water that has a muddy bottom in which it can bury itself when hibernating or when ambushing its prey.

This turtle is especially disliked by people who are interested in fish or birds. It is accused of eating fish that the fisherman might otherwise catch. Of course, the fish it eats are small, below the legal limit for the fisherman. However, the fisherman thinks they would grow up to become big fish. This idea has been demonstrated as false. For as long as there are too many small fish in a body of water, the limitation on the food supply

An American snapping turtle

will prevent larger ones from developing. It is true that the snapping turtle has been seen to pull ducklings underwater as prey, and there is one account of a turtle having bitten off the leg of an adult Canada goose. But people who condemn the snapper for this reason fail to realize that baby snappers are the natural prey of birds! The early years of a snapper's life are extremely hazardous. The nests are dug up and the eggs eaten by a great number of animals. Foxes, skunks, badgers, and raccoons all relish turtle eggs and know how to find them. Thus, 60 to 70 per cent of all nests are destroyed. And from the minute that the turtles hatch and hasten to the sheltering water, they are in danger. Most of them are eaten by such predators as herons, bitterns, gulls, muskrats, and even large turtles and fish.

It is only when the snapper has managed to survive for five or six years that it becomes large enough to defy these predators. It can then look forward to a life of some twenty-five to fifty years—provided it does not fall victim to some human, who either wants to make soup of it or thinks the poor turtle is an instrument of the devil.

Snapping turtles are well named. Unlike most turtles, which usually reach out slowly to their food, the snapper shoots out its long neck suddenly and snaps up whatever it is aiming for with a remarkably strong and sharp beak. It is this knifelike weapon that can sever a goose's leg or break an incautious finger. But snappers do not deserve their reputation for bad dispositions or wanton aggression. The urge to strike for food is innate, and can even be seen in baby turtles and in embryos inside the shell. The well-known turtle expert Dr. Archie Carr says that these turtles are only aggressive to man when on land. This is understandable, as they are at a disadvantage when out of the water and are put on the defensive. Once back in their natural element, they become docile. Even stepping on a turtle when wading does not result in lost toes. All the turtle will do is retreat into its shell.

The head of a snapping turtle

The snapper is not an especially large turtle. It can grow to
a length of three feet, but this includes the head and tail, both
remarkably long, so that the shell will be only slightly more than
a third of the length. A turtle this size can weigh as much as
fifty pounds. Besides its long neck and tail, it is recognized by
its loose, warty skin and its rough shell (when young), which
has three blunt ridges. In an old turtle, the shell is worn and
smooth. The undershell is quite small, which allows more room
for the legs to move, so that this turtle is very agile. The long
tail has horny crests on top and defensive shields on the underside. The color varies from light to dark brown, even black.
But since the snapper lives almost entirely in the water, the shell
is often covered with a growth of algae, which adds a greenish
tinge to the animal.

Besides its agility, its shell, and its powerful snapping beak,
the snapper has one other defense. This is a foul, musky odor.
When attacked or disturbed, the turtle often emits a yellow
liquid that has a disagreeable smell. This may discourage some
enemies. Once it has reached a fair size, the snapper has few
predators to fear besides man. But it may be killed during winter
hibernation if the temperature drops too low. Also, heavy snow
remaining too long on the ice can reduce the oxygen in the
water and thus wipe out the turtle population.

Although it was long believed that the snapping turtle was
mostly carnivorous, recent investigations have proved this to be
untrue. It turns out that this creature is truly omnivorous, like
man. One scientist found that his turtles preferred dead fish to
live ones. And aquatic vegetation makes up a large part of its
diet. One investigation turned up the following in nineteen
snapper stomachs: algae, leaves, seeds, grass, slugs, snails, cray-
fish, insects, bugs, flies, beetles, frogs, snakes, and portions of fish,
birds, mice, and rabbits. It seems that the snapper will eat anything
edible that comes its way. This fact might have been deduced
long ago from a practice of New England farmers, who would
put a snapper in their swill barrel (garbage can, to you) and

Young snapping turtles

leave it there to fatten for the table. One such turtle is said to have reached a weight of eighty-six pounds!

Snappers often come together in large numbers to hibernate. But once spring arrives, and they crawl out of the muddy bottom, they wander off separately. Mating takes place any time between April and November, varying with the climate. But this activity is seldom observed as it usually happens underwater. The male climbs on top of the female and keeps his balance by clinging to her shell with the claws of his four feet.

A few battles between males have been observed, but whether they were over a female or a territory is not known. Most females dig their nests and lay their eggs in June, but some have been known to wait until as late as October. In such a case, the eggs probably overwinter and hatch the next spring.

Females often wander a good distance in search of the right nesting place, and often dig several false nests before making their final choice. They must have soft soil to dig in. Sometimes the female turtle will emit a quantity of water from her body to help soften the earth. Often she makes her nest in a soft bank. She digs her way in until she is almost buried and then lays her eggs. When she backs out, the dirt of the bank falls down and covers the eggs.

Harold Babcock, in his book *Turtles of the Northeastern United States,* quotes an interesting observation of such egg laying in the year 1911, noted by the late Professor J. W. P. Jenks. The professor's turtle was "about the size of a big scoop-shovel," and she came out of the pond with a fixed purpose and moved inland. The professor realized what she was up to and followed her. In order not to alarm her, he followed her on all fours—like another turtle. She led him across the sand, up a cow path, under fence rails, and through a pasture that was full of wet vines and briars.

"She was laying her course, I thought, straight down the length of this dreadful pasture, when, not far from the fence, she suddenly hove to, warped herself short about, and came back, barely clearing me, at a clip that was thrilling. I warped about, too, and in her wake bore down across the corner of the pasture, across the powdery public road (this was before the days of cement highways!) and on to a fence along a field of young corn . . . Hurrying up behind a large tree by the fence, I peered down the corn rows and saw the turtle stop and begin to paw about in the loose soil . . . she tried this place and that place and the other place . . . But *the* place, evidently, was hard to find. What could a female turtle do with a whole field of possible nests to choose from? Then at last she found it, and whirling about, she backed quickly at it and, tail first, began to bury herself before my staring eyes."

Because of its wide distribution across North America, the snapping turtle seems in no danger of extinction, as is the case with its seagoing relative, the green turtle. But when men condemn it as a greedy predator, they might well remember that the most destructive animal on the planet today is the human species.

6

The Turkey Vulture
(Cathartes aura)

"Dirty old buzzard!" This is the least of the abuse hurled at the turkey vulture, that magnificent master of the American skies. No bird is as skillful a glider over land or can continue for so long. The bird soars with hardly a flick of its huge wings upon the thermal updrafts—rising currents of warm air. But because the buzzard feeds only on dead animals, and thus reminds us of death, it is shunned and hated.

Yet the vulture (or buzzard, as it is popularly known in the United States) does not kill to eat, as does the eagle—a much more honored bird. It does not have the eagle's formidable equipment of strong claws and powerful beak. The buzzard's claws are too weak and dull to seize live prey and its beak is so blunt, compared to that of hawks and eagles, that it cannot carve up a carcass until the sun has had a softening effect.

Because the buzzard is slow to start in on a meal and is often seen sitting around a carcass, it has been called a coward. In

47

reality, it is waiting for the sun to cook its dinner. The buzzard is not a bird of death; it merely cleans up after death has had its way.

The turkey buzzard got its name because its head and neck are bare of feathers, as is the case with the turkey. And its skin is mottled red and blue, also like the turkey gobbler. In this case, nature seems to have gone out of her way to be sure that the buzzard would not be a dirty bird. A fully feathered bird might well dirty itself with the buzzard's diet, but food does not adhere to that naked head and neck.

In contrast to the colorful head, the buzzard's body feathers are brownish-black. Its six-foot wingspread is so great that the wings must cross behind the square tail when the bird is grounded. And its eyesight is so keen that it has been referred to as telescopic vision.

A turkey buzzard

There is some speculation as to whether the vulture finds its food entirely by sight, or if it also uses its sense of smell. Edward Howe Forbush, in his *Natural History of the Birds of Eastern and Central North America,* says that vultures have large nostrils and therefore probably possess a sense of smell. He notes that sometimes they fail to locate their food if it is concealed by a thin covering, like paper. But on the other hand, they have been seen to hover over a decaying body that was hidden by something like a bush. This would indicate that perhaps the bird smelled the carcass it could not see.

This bird can be found almost anywhere in America as far north as New England and occasionally up into Canada. It spends the summer in the north, but goes south in the winter, for it needs the updrafts of warm air in order to maintain its soaring flight; and frozen, snow-covered country would make difficult hunting for a scavenger.

Buzzards come north with the spring. In the village of Hinckley, Ohio, they are welcomed as joyfully as returning swallows. For 150 years, and perhaps long before men began to count the time, the buzzards of Hinckley have returned to their roosting ledges on March 15, and for the past fifteen years they have been welcomed by an ever growing crowd of fans. By 1968 more than 40,000 people were coming to Hinckley to see the buzzards return, and the Chamber of Commerce now declares a buzzard festival on that date. So far, the birds have never let them down.

Buzzards migrate in flocks, but once arrived, they tend to nest in pairs. They are large birds and need large nesting places, and suitable sites are not always easily found. They like steep cliffs, which can only be reached from the air. Sometimes they nest in caves or hollow stumps or thick shrubs that serve to discourage an enemy. They do little to make the nest soft and comfortable, often laying their eggs right on the ground or on the stones of a cliff. If the nest is in a hollow stump, they may pull off pieces of the rotten wood and tear them to bits to spread on the floor of the nest. Both birds help with this work, and observers have watched them standing in the nest with their heads close together. Sometimes, when the male bird got in her way, the female would give him a push, and on one occasion he was seen to fall out of the nest. However, he was soon back again, lending moral support to his mate.

Usually, two dull or creamy white eggs are laid. These are marked with spots and splashes of varying shades of brown. It takes nearly thirty days for them to hatch, and another eight to ten weeks before the young birds are able to fly. While they are still small, the parent birds regurgitate food for the nestlings, opening wide their beaks while the offspring reach in for the food. In this way, the young birds learn to associate the smell of decomposing meat with the idea of a good dinner.

Young buzzards raised in captivity soon learn to recognize their keeper. They will poke their beaks into a partially closed hand in search of food, possibly an instinctive substitute for thrusting inside the parent's bill. They seem to enjoy being handled and petted and will follow the keeper about like a dog. Buzzards communicate by hissing, a low hiss meaning pleasure and a louder, more forceful one, anger.

The most remarkable attribute of the turkey buzzard is its ability to soar for seemingly endless periods, with rarely a flap of its wings. This is achieved by the great wingspread and also by the formation of those wings, which are uptilted at the ends to make a flattened V. This position of the wings, called "dihedral," gives the bird stability and keeps it from rolling over as it soars. If you want to distinguish a buzzard from a hawk or an eagle, watch for the gliding, flapless flight and also for that flattened V of the wings.

Buzzards are expert at locating the updrafts of heated air and soaring skyward. People who practice the sport of gliding often look for a buzzard and use the same updraft to promote their flight. Buzzards seem to have no objection to a human glider in their midst. Often there may be as many as ten buz-

Turkey buzzards

zards sailing upward on the same air current. Once they are
high aloft, where they can look down on the countryside, each
buzzard will cover a certain area, watching for any sign of a
dead animal. (Usually there are no more than two or three
buzzards to a square mile.) But should one buzzard drop down
to earth to investigate a possible meal, it will be quickly followed
by the buzzards nearest to it in the sky. Those birds will bring
others after them, so that soon there will be a dozen or more
gathered about the carcass.

Animals killed on the highway are a likely meal for buzzards
today. But John Terres, in his *Adventures with Vultures,* tells of
a forest near his boyhood home, which once was used as a dump-
ing ground for dead horses. "Horse Heaven," as the place was

called, was kept clean by vultures, which quickly disposed of the remains. Watching these big birds perform was one experience that started Mr. Terres on a career of bird study.

The turkey buzzard has two American relatives. The largest, the condor, with wings ten feet across, is becoming extinct. There are only a few of these great birds left in the Southwest, and conservationists are working hard to save them. But the outcome is doubtful. Only forty or fifty are still alive in a protected section of the California coast.

The other, the black vulture, lives in our southern states. It has smaller wings and must flap more frequently to stay aloft. For this reason it keeps to the South, where thermal updrafts are stronger. It is a more aggressive bird than the turkey buzzard, and has been known to drive the latter from a carcass. It also will kill small animals, such as skunks and newborn piglets, which turkey buzzards do not do.

People who have studied and worked with the buzzard claim that it is an intelligent bird. An example of its remarkable ability to adapt was noticed first in 1935 by a well-known duck bander. One day when he was working in a field, he noticed an airplane flying toward him. Then he thought he was seeing two airplanes —until they passed overhead, when he saw that the second was a vulture, gliding close behind the plane. He observed this unusual behavior on several occasions, but not until twenty years later was the mystery solved. Then it was realized that the big bird was doing what wild geese and swans do when on migration. These birds fly in the famous V formation, so that each following bird takes advantage of the slipstream of air from the wing of the bird ahead. The buzzard had been doing the same with the airplane—getting a free ride on the air that was stirred up by its passage.

7

The Red Bat
(Lasiurus borealis)

Misunderstandings about bats go back a very long time. In fact, even today the uninformed may think that bats are birds. And it was not until this century that some of the most fascinating facts about these mammals were uncovered.

Medieval folklore is full of horrendous tales about bats, which were believed to be evil, unclean, and associated with the devil. In more recent and enlightened times, they were supposed to make a practice of nesting in women's hair.

As eminent a scientist as Linnaeus was, he too was at first confused about bats. He noted the many similarities between bats and men: the skeletal formations and the fact that there are only two teats, placed between the forelimbs. Only in men, monkeys, bats, elephants, and a few such rare species is this found. Consequently, Linneaus at first placed bats in the order of Primates, which includes men, monkeys, and apes. But after due thought, he realized that this was not right and set up a special order for

53

the flying mammals, calling them Chiroptera, meaning hand-winged.

Bats have been associated with men since very ancient times, when men lived in caves. In all probability, the bats were already there, for their ancestry goes back millions of years. Bats were already bats fifty or sixty million years ago, whereas man's lineage goes back a scant million years. Thus, when men began to seek shelter in caves, they found they must accept these little flying mammals as neighbors. And today, when men have built their own "caves" in the form of houses, bats have a tendency to follow them there. Houses have many nooks and crannies where a bat can sleep away the day.

However, man is a daytime animal, and bats sleep by day and fly at night. These strangs flitting shapes that appeared with the threatening dark gave rise to all sorts of terrors and superstitions. And bats, for most people, have always been associated with dark and dismal beliefs. Only in the East—especially in China— have bats appeared in a more cheerful light. In the Chinese language the word for bat is *fu,* and the symbol for *fu* is the same as the symbol for happiness. For this reason, bats are taken as omens of good fortune. The bat is used extensively in designs on pottery, in jade carving, and in art of all sorts. Orientals often wear a pendant, called a *wu-fu,* that shows five bats arranged in a circle facing inward with wings outspread. This, they believe, is a token of good luck and long life for the wearer.

Bats are found on all the continents except Antarctica. While they are essentially tropical animals, they have spread out to cover much of the northern latitudes. When winter comes to these regions, the bats have different ways of dealing with the problem. Some species migrate to warmer climates, often traveling the same routes and in company with the birds. Other species of bats hibernate. They do this often in a cave, which may be used year after year.

On the other hand, many bats use caves for sleeping during daylight hours and issue forth in a huge swarm at evening, when they disperse on their nightly hunt for insects. Almost all of our bats in America are insect eaters, with the exception of a few fruit or nectar eaters, which may wander across the border from Mexico. In this, they are very useful animals, serving to keep down the populations of many destructive insects.

The bat is famous for its quick, darting flight and sudden turns, a mode of flight developed in its constant pursuit of insects. But how the bat can find and pursue its prey in the darkest night was a mystery until the present century. With the development of electronics—radio, radar, and recording techniques—it was possible to study sounds outside the range of the human ear. It was then discovered that bats had already invented radar—an instrument that men have only recently developed for use in war, aviation, and weather sciences.

As the bat flies, it makes little squeaks. These squeaks are so high-pitched that we cannot hear them, but the bat can hear them, and can also hear the echoes as they bounce off any obstacles ahead of it. The bat's ears are so acute that it can be said to see with its ears. It not only "sees" when something is ahead of it, but it "sees" what it is. It sees well enough with its radar

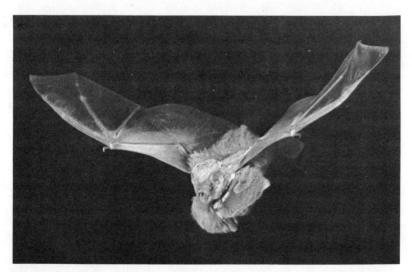

A red bat carrying her young

to be able to find and chase insects, which are also doing flying acrobatics in their efforts to escape. This remarkable radar of the bats makes it hard to catch them in nets, as is done with birds for scientific study. Bats can "see" the nets in the dark, and only especially fine "mist nets," devised by the Japanese, have proved equal to the task of catching bats for "bat-banding."

Many bats have peculiar growths on their faces, especially on the nose. There are leaf-nosed bats and spear-nosed bats and bats with strangely shaped ears. It is believed that most of these grotesque decorations are refinements of their radar system. For to navigate properly, the bat must listen only to its own echo, and often there are thousands of other bats around, all squeaking and making their own echoes. Furthermore, to operate radar properly, the receiver must be shut off when the sound is sent out, so that only the echo is picked up. It has been found that the bat does this with a little muscle inside its ear. When the bat squeaks, the muscle contracts, closing the ear. Then the muscle relaxes, allowing the bat to hear only the echo.

Some of the strangest bats live in the tropics and are not met with in the American night. In Australia and Southeast Asia there are huge bats with a wingspread of some fifty inches. In Germany the bat is called a flying mouse (*Fledermaus*). But in Australia the bats are known as flying foxes! These are mostly fruit bats, and they gather in large flocks in trees (called camps) and are said to be very noisy and often destructive to orchards. In South America there are many bats of weird appearance, including the vampire bat. This bat lives on the blood of other animals and can be a threat to domestic herds. It has two specially adapted, razor-sharp front teeth with which it makes a shallow cut in the victim's skin. Then it drinks the flowing blood with its tongue. It can do this without awakening the person or animal.

It has been estimated that a colony of 100 vampire bats can take 186 gallons of blood a year from domestic animals in their area, as well as preying occasionally on wild animals. More seriously, these bats carry the dreaded rabies virus, which they transmit to any creature that they bite. Strangely, the bats remain immune to the disease. The U.N. Food and Agriculture Organization says that about two million cattle (worth $100 million) and at least a half-dozen humans die each year in Latin America because of vampire bats. Extensive research is now underway to find a means of controlling these, the only dangerous bats.

Bats specialize in their food patterns, as do birds and ants and many other creatures. Bats that eat insects do not eat fruit, and fruit bats do not drink blood. There are several other specializations, such as the tropical bats with thin noses or long tongues that seek out flowers, usually on tall trees. They feed on the nectar or pollen and, like the humming bird, do a useful job of fertilizing the plants at the same time. And there are the bats that eat fish, and have learned to catch them by flying low over a pond or stream and grabbing them with their claws.

One of America's more colorful bats is the red bat, a medium-sized bat with thick, heavy fur and long, pointed wings. We think of most bats as being some dull shade of brown, but this species is colored bright orange or yellow-brown or shades in between. The males are apt to be more colorful than the females. They can be found from southern Canada through our eastern states and south into Mexico, and also in the west through California and north to British Columbia and Alberta, Canada. They are seldom found in Florida, but are especially abundant in the Middle West and the Ohio River valley.

They do not congregate in great flocks, as do many species of bats, being solitary rather than social. They spend the daytime hanging among the leaves of trees in small groups, or sometimes singly, or a mother with babies. Hanging from a leaf or a twig with its wings folded around it, this bat looks much like a dead leaf. Usually, a bunch of leaves is selected, from four to ten feet above the ground, where the surrounding leafy canopy gives protection on all sides, screening out the light and concealing the bat. But there must also be a clear space beneath, so that the bat can drop straight down when commencing its flight. There must also be a lack of any lower branches from which enemies might see the sleeping bats.

Red bats come out of hiding early in the evening. At first they fly slowly, high in the air, and seem to be playing. But after about a half hour they descend to tree level and begin flying purposefully in search of insects, often only a few feet above the ground. They are one of the species that frequent street lights as a source of insect food, and they have been found to eat flies, beetles, bugs, cicadas, and even crickets. The last suggests that they sometimes catch their food on the ground.

Mating takes place in August—and unlike most other bats, in the air! Observers have seen these bats come together in flight and continue to fly together for a short time. However, as with many bats, fertilization does not occur immediately. The male sperm is stored in the female's uterus throughout the winter when the bats are in hibernation. The female's egg is fertilized in the spring, and the babies are born some eighty to ninety days later. These baby bats are very small and are born without hair and with their eyes closed. Most bats have one or two offspring, but the red bat, perhaps because it is so small, may have as many as four. Three is the average. They cling to the mother's fur until they are strong enough to be left hanging in a roost while she hunts for food.

As with most bats, the mother has the entire care of the young. During this time, the males and females tend to live apart. The young are weaned early and can fly within a few weeks. Observers have seen young bats, left hanging at the roost by the mother, go through a variety of exercises, stretching their wings and trying their muscles in preparation for flight.

It is believed that red bats migrate, moving from the north to more southern sections of the country. Several red bats have been found among the thousands of birds killed annually by hitting the Empire State Building and television towers. That fewer bats than birds suffer these accidents is undoubtedly due to the bats' remarkable radar.

The red bat, *Lasiurus borealis,* is not only a migratory bat. It also hibernates. These bats are known to spend the winter in the Ohio River valley, as well as in such states as Kentucky and Virginia. In all these states winter temperatures often fall well below freezing. Although red bats are heavily furred, they cannot be active at temperatures much below 66 degrees F. Moreover, unless the temperature rises this high, they cannot find food, as no insects will be flying.

While red bats have been known to enter caves and have been captured there, most of them hibernate in trees. In fact, scientists believe that these bats are so well adapted to survival outdoors that they would be unable to survive in caves. The slight changes in cave temperatures would not be sufficient to arouse them from dormancy. They are well adapted to survival in subfreezing cold by their heavy fur, which covers all except their ears and parts of their wings. The ears are short and round, to conserve heat, and the furry interfemoral membrane (between the legs) is used as a blanket.

The hibernation of bats is one aspect now being studied by scientists. While the bat's radar is one of the greatest of animal mysteries that modern science has explained, there are many other attributes of these little mammals that are almost as puzzling. One fact is that this animal can lower its body temperature, heartbeat, and breathing rate so that it can live for months without eating, in a kind of cold storage. This may account for the remarkable longevity of some species of bats. All animal species have a certain life span, with the general rule that the smaller the animal, the shorter its life, and the larger the animal, the longer. Thus, mice have a life expectancy of about a year, dogs of about ten years, and elephants of about fifty. However, the bat, some species of which are smaller than a mouse, often live for fifteen years! A banded bat was recovered after twenty-three years, and large fruit bats (which do not hibernate) have been known to live nineteen years in captivity. What's more, the insect-eating bats do this on a diet of fatty insects. Scientists have found no great difference in the arteries of a young bat and one that is twenty years old. How this happens is a matter of great interest to doctors working in the fields of human heart and circulatory illnesses.

Scientists are also studying how the bat manages to store the male sperm in the female uterus and effect fertilization at a later date. This knowledge may lead to medical breakthroughs in problems of human infertility and to better artificial insemination for domestic animals. And finally, the bat's radar is a never-ending wonder. Their echo-location system is thought to be far more sensitive and efficient than any of our radar and sonar devices. Experimenting scientists once hung twenty-eight hairlike wires in a dark room where bats were flying. Then they turned on seventy loudspeakers producing a noise 2,000 times stronger than the bat's squeak and on the same frequency. None of this bothered the bats! They flew through the maze of wires without difficulty.

Bats have also been found to have a homing navigational device similar to that of pigeons. When taken from their daytime roosts and moved as much as sixty miles away, they have flown back in one night.

There are many accounts of people who have had pet bats. They are usually scientists or naturalists. At first, even when the bats became tame enough to take food from the hand, they usually died after a few months. Now many scientists and zoos have learned how to keep them alive in captivity for years. Scientists studying hibernating bats keep them in refrigerators, with a sign on the door reading "Sleeping Bats, Do Not Disturb." When they are needed for study, they are brought out and awakened.

Bats are far more useful than they are harmful. Their greatest threat to man is as carriers of disease. It has long been known that the bats of South America harbor rabies. Rabies can be spread from bat to bat, and while we in the

United States do not need to fear the vampire bat, in the past few decades it has been found that some of our native bats have the dreaded disease.

Rabies is endemic among most of our wild animals, and there are periodic outbreaks of epidemic proportions. Many dogs, if not inoculated and if allowed to run loose, can contract the disease, for which there is no cure. However, nobody suggests that all dogs should be killed because a few of them get rabies. And it would be as foolish to suggest the same for bats. One should remember never to pick up a bat that appears to be sick or is acting strangely. And the same holds true for other wild animals and for strange dogs. Vampire bats are now being studied in the laboratory and have been trained to come to a small dish to feed, lapping up blood obtained from a slaughterhouse.

Bats are not yet among the endangered species of animals, and with their worldwide distribution it would seem that they are not likely to become extinct in the near future. Nevertheless, with man's penetration of every corner of the planet and with our efforts to exterminate injurious insects, a great falling off of the bat population of the United States has been noted in the last two decades. At one time there were millions of bats in the Carlsbad Caverns, and now there are hardly any. There are probably several reasons for this, but the true cause has not yet been determined.

Bats are apt to move their roosting places if disturbed, and the number of people visiting these caverns has increased with the years. Bats also move if there is a change of climate. Thus, a drought that caused a great decrease in the insect population would encourage the bats to look elsewhere for food. Finally, the overall use of DDT as an insecticide, which has killed so many birds and animals, may also have killed the bats. Some people argue that bats catch their prey on the wing and so would not be eating poisoned insects. However, bats have sometimes been seen to take prey on the ground, and some

Bats in flight

poisoned insects might still fly a bit before dying. If the DDT did not poison the bats directly, it certainly removed their food supply. At any rate, it is probably good that our government has finally placed a ban upon this miracle poison that turned out to be more of a menace.

Scientists studying bats are beginning to urge that attention be given to their protection and conservation. In addition to the threats already mentioned, there has been a big increase in the sport of speleology (cave exploration), and such activities must necessarily disturb the bats that have lived in the caves for centuries. This interrupts their breeding and their life cycle. Since the majority of bats produce only one offspring a season, such continued disturbance must work to cut down their numbers.

Bat scientists urge that people going into caves make every effort not to disturb the bats unless they have some legitimate, scientific purpose. It would be a pity if this remarkable animal should disappear forever and take with it the many secrets of its wonderful pattern of life.

8

The Porcupine
(*Erethizon dorsatum*)

Is it possible for the porcupine to be misunderstood? Everyone knows it as a walking menace, an animal best let alone. How can there be any misunderstanding about that? Surely, the only misunderstanding occurs when a nosy dog gets too close and receives a snoutful of quills.

The truth of the matter is that the porcupine's horrendous reputation keeps people at such a distance that few realize what a remarkable beast the North American porcupine really is. As a matter of fact, the porcupine is one of the most unusual characters in the animal world and on occasion has even become a beloved pet.

To begin with, porky has one of the best defense systems of all animals. Those quills—30,000 of them on one porcupine! —can do so much damage that their reputation has become inflated. Many people believe that a porcupine can throw its quills. This is untrue. When threatened, the animal turns its

63

A porcupine

back and raises its quills so that it seems twice its true size, with the barbs all pointing at the enemy. It lashes its tail back and forth, and whenever it hits anything, a dozen quills fly off, giving the impression that the porcupine is throwing them. Any animal rash enough to come within range of that thrashing tail will receive a handful of quills in its face. These work their way into the flesh and are very painful to extract. Bears, mountain lions, and other predators have died of starvation because their mouths and throats were clogged with porcupine quills.

One animal clever enough to make a meal of the porcupine is the fisher. This North American member of the weasel family has learned to reach under the little quill pig with impunity and deftly flip it over on its back. Then it grabs the unprotected stomach before the animal can right itself. The wolverine and the great horned owl are two other enemies that the porcupine must fear.

Undoubtedly, the porcupine's greatest enemy is man, for some of its habits have put it on the list of forest pests. The animal's favorite food is the bark of trees, especially in the winter months when the vegetation on the forest floor is under a blanket of snow. The porcupine finds a comfortable perch in a tasty tree and stays there, often for several days, nibbling on the bark. It is the juicy underbark that is favored, and this is what conducts the sap and nutrition from the leaves down to the roots and back again. If the porcupine eats all the way around it, the tree will die. Naturally, this habit does not endear it to foresters.

Another failing of the beast is that it is fanatically fond of salt. Any item that has been handled by a man with sweaty hands will taste salty enough to a porcupine to start him chewing on it. And those sharp rodent teeth that can girdle a tree find no difficulty in chewing up such things as canoe paddles, tabletops, saddle leather, and innumerable items of camping equipment.

For these misdeeds, as well as for its menace to dogs and other domestic animals, the porcupine has had a bad reputation with woodsmen and for many years was shot on sight. Now that it has become rare in some areas, many states have made it a protected animal. For in spite of its faults in human eyes, it is an unusual and interesting animal, and it would be regrettable if it were entirely eradicated from our wilds.

The porcupine is a northern animal and can withstand cold better than heat. It is mostly found in forests north of the 40th parallel, although there is a yellow species that lives in the southwestern states. It grows to be thirty inches long and six inches of that is tail. It weighs from fifteen to twenty-five pounds, and as it waddles slowly through the woods, its 30,000 quills rattle as it walks. Those quills are so light that they act like a life preserver in the water and keep it afloat as it swims across rivers. They also act like a cushion if the animal falls out of a tree. And baby porkies often do so before they learn the art of descending a tree backward.

Contrary to some opinion, porcupines are quite vocal. Otis H. Green, writing in *Nature Magazine,* describes the love-making of two porcupines in a tree near his camp in the Adirondacks. He says that the squalling and caterwauling that went on would have put an alley cat to shame. When Mr. Green crept close to the tree to discover the source of the disturbance, the animals quieted to a faint grumbling, whimpering, and chattering of teeth. In the summer dusk he could make out the two porcupines high up in a tall tree. It was his opinion that most of the noise was made by the female, perched higher in the tree and calling her mate up to her.

Many people have wondered how two such prickly animals ever get together for the mating process, and some have suggested that it is done face to face in order to avoid the quills. However, scientists assure us that their mating is done in the usual fashion, with the male approaching the female from the rear and above. The noted naturalist Jean Craighead George, in her book *Beastly Inventions,* states that the porcupine is the only mammal that does not grab hold of his female. She says that they do not touch quills and that their matings are brief and infrequent. It has also been noted that the female is careful to keep her barbed tail out of the way.

Another cause for wonder is how the female manages to give birth to her prickly baby. For little porcupines are born fully quilled and able to defend themselves. As a rule, only one baby is born, but that one is remarkably large. It often weighs more than a pound at birth, while the mother may weigh between twelve and twenty pounds. A black bear cub is smaller at birth than a baby porcupine! This makes the porcupine baby one of the largest of any of the mammals in porportion to the mother.

As you can see, the infant porcupine is well developed when it is born. Its quills are soft at first, and as it is born wrapped in a membrane covering, the mother seems to have no difficulty. Although the baby is born in a den of sorts—a hole or a hollow log—it is soon ready to follow its mother about and learn from her the choice of foods. It is nursed for only three weeks, and in a few months is able to take care of itself. Occasionally, albinos are born, and these all-white porcupines make interesting zoo exhibits.

Indians of our Southwest have long respected the porcupine, and its quills are used to decorate a variety of things, from canoes to weapons, from moccasins to headdresses. The porcupine does not miss the quills that are shed, for it quickly grows replacements.

Still, even after these considerations, who would imagine that the porcupine could make a satisfactory pet? But this is the opinion of scientists who have studied the animal, as well as outdoors people who have happened to fall heir to a baby quill pig. This last was the case of Ronald Rood, the well-known nature writer.

Rood came upon his baby porcupine after a forest fire.

A porcupine

The unfortunate animal had lost its mother in the blaze. It approached the men, crying because the hot ashes had burned its feet. It would have taken a hard heart to abandon the orphan, but nobody wanted to pick it up! Then someone scooped it up with a shovel, dumped it into a coat, and so carried it to their car.

When they got him home to the Rood farm and into a box, they found that the frightened animal would not eat, although they offered him all sorts of vegetable goodies. Finally, they decided to try milk, which would have to be fed to him with an eyedropper. Rood put on a heavy coat and gloves, turned the baby quill pig on its back, and prepared to play substitute for a mother porcupine. The poor baby was very frightened. He held his little black claws over his nose (the porcupine's weakest spot) and shut his eyes tightly. But the minute the warm milk trickled over his mouth, he stopped resisting. He grabbed the eyedropper with both paws and sucked it dry. After that, there were no more feeding problems.

In fact, there were no more problems at all—for the baby porcupine. He lost all fear of his human friends and was soon following them about. He quickly learned his name and would come running when called, asking to be picked up and petted. Apparently, as long as the animal is not frightened, its quills lie flat, buried among the long hairs, and if you stroke it the same way that the quills lie, there is no danger. Picking one up is something of a trick. The Roods learned to slide their hands underneath Pokey (as the orphan was named) and pick him up by his soft underpart.

At first the Rood children wondered how a young porcupine would play, and they soon found out. One day after he had finished a good meal, Pokey began to dance. In fact, Rood describes it as a war dance. First the porcupine arched his back like a cat, which raised his quills menacingly. Then he whirled about, several turns one way and several turns in reverse. Then he ran backward with his tail swinging, and finally he did several stiff-legged hops, before going into his whirling dance again.

As long as he was little, there was no problem about giving Pokey the run of the house, and he was soon everybody's pet. He even got along well with the shepherd dog, climbing up on its back for a ride. And Rood used to let him ride back and forth on the carriage of his typewriter while he was working. But one night the Roods were awakened by strange sounds from the kitchen. Going to investigate, they found Pokey having fun on the kitchen table. He had sampled the butter and a bowl of apples, but after that he had started in on the kitchen table, chewing right through the tablecloth to get at the wood.

This episode put an end to Pokey's days as a house guest. Rood built a cage for him, after all suggestions that he be sent to a zoo or released in the wild had been strenuously rejected by the Rood children. He would not last long in the wilds, they pointed out, for he would walk right up to a hunter and his dog in trusting innocence.

Pokey did not like confinement in the cage. He objected noisily, first with a good imitation of a barking dog, then with frantic squealing and wailing. Finally, he gave vent to pathetic sniffles that were more moving than the louder protests. In practice, he did not stay long in the cage, for somebody was always taking him out for a romp.

Whatever the problems of raising a porcupine may be, Rood wrote a fascinating article about his little pet.

So it would seem that porcupines have been misunderstood after all. They are far more interesting and rewarding animals than any of us have suspected.

9

The Pig
(Sus scrofa)

Throughout history, the epithet "pig" has been one of the worst insults hurled at an adversary. And today, in the heat of confrontation, the use of this animal's name all too often leads to violence and to jail sentences. For to call a person a pig is to imply that he or she is dirty and greedy and altogether a beast of a lower order.

Why do people have such a low opinion of the pig? Is there any truth in the accusations? The first question may be hard to answer. But the second is easy. The answer on all counts is, No!

The farmer puts the pig in a small, cramped pen, dusty in dry weather and muddy in wet, and then wonders why the animal is dirty. In his book *Animals Nobody Loves,* Ronald Rood tells the story of two pigs that were raised on his farm from the time they were piglets. One day, at the suggestion of a neighbor, he threw some hay into the bare pigpen. To his

A pig

astonishment, the two pigs went wild with joy. They threw the hay into the air, playing with it and rolling in it. Then they collected it all into one corner, where they made themselves a nest of the clean, fresh hay. For the rest of the summer, Rood saw to it that they had new hay several times a week. And the pigs kept their sleeping quarters clean. They went to defecate in a spot at the opposite corner of the pen. In reality, the pig is as clean an animal as the cat is.

When it comes to food, the pig is omnivorous, like man. For this reason, the practice has been to feed it the poorest and dirtiest rations. The pig will eat almost anything when it is hungry. But it can tell the difference between good food and bad, and it will root around in its trough to find the better morsels. This often results in the food being strewn all over the pen and adds to the impression that the pig is dirty. However, the pig knows when it has eaten its fill and then it stops. This is quite different from the horse and the cow. Both these animals will eat themselves sick if given the chance. It might be more accurate to say "greedy as a cow," than "greedy as a pig."

Then there is the general belief that pigs are stupid. This also turns out to be a fallacy. Pigs have been trained to do a great variety of things, from performing tricks in the circus to retrieving like a dog. The French king Louis XI used to cheer himself up by watching a performance of dancing pigs.

During the Middle Ages in England, when the common people were forbidden to keep dogs in the New Forest, pigs were sometimes used for hunting. In those times, poor people were only allowed to hunt small game, such as rabbits and birds. The deer were the property of the king and the nobility, and it was feared that large dogs would chase the deer.

Thus, people living near the New Forest were forbidden to have any but the smallest dogs. There was a special stirrup, 10½ by 7½ inches in size, through which the dog must be able to creep in order to qualify. Any animal that could not get through the stirrup was banned. However, you could keep a large dog as a guard, if you had him "expedited." This meant that several toes were cut off the dog's front feet, thus crippling the animal so that it could no longer run fast and be a threat to the deer.

In this emergency, pigs were trained not only to retrieve the game when shot but also to smell it out and go into a point, showing the hunter where the prey was hidden.

Another unusual use to which the pig has been put is searching for truffles. Pigs are natural rooting animals, pushing their snouts under leaves and logs and stones to smell out acorns and other delicacies of the forest floor. Truffles, the black mushrooms that grow in Italy and France, are the delight of gourmets and are highly prized. As they are not easily found, pigs are often used to help in the search. A muzzle is placed around the pig's nose, so that it cannot eat the truffles, and as soon as one is nosed out, the truffle digger places it in his basket.

Undoubtedly, the greatest service rendered by the pig is the production of food for man. In this it far outstrips cattle or sheep. One third of what the pig eats goes into meat, but only one eighth in the case of sheep and cattle. And pigs multiply faster than any other barnyard animal. As a relatively small animal, it is easily transported and can be kept in a small space: a pen or even in the house, as was often done in China.

Pigs were brought to this continent by Columbus and they played a part in the opening of the West. The pioneers took pigs along beside their covered wagons. They could live off the land, run and leap like any horse, survive storms and freezing weather, and even fight off a wolf if necessary.

Scientists recognize two major divisions of the pig family: the European wild pig (*Sus scrofa*) and the Asiatic pig (*Sus vittatus*), which was domesticated by the Chinese in ancient times and has spread throughout the East. There are many intermediate species, and there has been so much interbreeding that it is now believed there is some Chinese blood in all domestic pigs.

A wild boar

As with the dog, man has bred many types of pigs. Some with long legs and some with short. Some large and some small. Pigs were not domesticated until men began to live in settled communities with the development of farming. For pigs are not easily herded, as are cattle, goats, and sheep. But once the agricultural revolution got under way, the pig became an important part of man's family of animals. In Neolithic times a group of people built their homes out on the lakes of Switzerland, probably as a means of defense against attack. At these sites archaeologists have dug up the bones of a small, delicate pig that may have been bred especially to live in the lake dwellings.

From these early times onward, the pig has been an important asset to man. Pig skeletons have been found in the excavations at Troy, and paintings and carvings of the animal have turned up in the ruins of Sumer, Egypt, and Greece. In Egypt they were put to work, as well as being used for food. Mural paintings show pigs at work, "treading the seed." Their small, pointed feet made holes of the proper depth to ensure germination.

In later periods the Egyptians associated the pig with one of their gods of evil, and it was believed that the souls of the wicked passed into pigs. F. E. Zeuner, in his *History of Domesticated Animals,* suggests that perhaps the Mosaic taboos against eating pork came from these Egyptian beliefs. Although the pig was highly esteemed in the ancient world, and a delicacy on the tables of Greece and Rome, some peoples, such as the Jews and the Arabs, have always had strong laws against eating it. For them, pigs are unclean. Historians are not agreed about where this idea originated, but one suggestion is interesting. Most of these peoples were originally nomadic, herding their flocks of goats or sheep from one good pasture to another. Such people are usually proud and aloof, and look down on the tribes that live in settled communities and practice agriculture. Thus they grew to despise

the farmer's pig as they despised the man who bred it. And all
this led eventually to a religious taboo against eating the
animal.

It now seems that the pig, the animal we have labeled
dirty, greedy, and stupid, is very much like the human species.
After our cousins, the apes and the monkeys, the pig is physi-
cally more like man than any other animal. Its digestive tract,
its heart and circulatory system, and even its teeth are much
like ours. It suffers from many of our ailments and diseases,
and for this reason it is now becoming a laboratory animal.
A special small strain of pig has recently been developed for
easy handling in the laboratory, and scientists experiment with
it to find new cures for TB, heart ailments, and even allergies.

The pig has come a long way, from the ancient forests
where it was chased by hunters to the modern laboratory
where it helps increase the miracles of modern medicine. But
there is one place in our country where you can still see the
wild European boar in all its glory. That is in the Appalachian
Mountains of North Carolina and Tennessee.

A group of these boars were brought over from Germany
in 1912 by a man who wanted to supply hunting excitement
for visiting English businessmen. The animals, at first kept on
a private game refuge, eventually escaped into the thickets and
tangles that the mountain people call "laurel hells." This was
a fine habitat for *Sus scrofa,* and the herds increased. The
mountaineers did not like the beasts. They had pigs of their
own running free, with which the wild boars mated. The tame
sows often ran off to join the wild herd, and when the farmers
were able to round them up, they found that the crossbred pigs
would not fatten nicely for market. Like their wild ancestors,
they would eat only enough to satisfy their hunger.

Eventually, the mountaineers were evicted to make way for
the national forest, and now there is no longer the problem of
crossbreeding with domestic pigs. These wild boars hardly
look like the conventional idea of a pig. They have a heavy

A collared peccary

coat of hair, which may be colored reddish-brown or black. They have a bristly mane atop heavy shoulders and both sexes have tusks. The wild boar has few enemies besides man (in the hunting season), for when cornered, it puts up a vicious battle and even a bear is no match for it. In the fifty years since their introduction, the Appalachian boars have increased from 14 to an estimated 1,200 animals.

Although wild boars and domestic pigs were both imported into this country by man, we do have a native species related to them. These are the little peccaries of our Southwest. Known as jabalinas or javelinas, they are smaller than the average boar, weighing from thirty-five to sixty-six pounds when grown. But they have many of the qualities of their larger cousins. They can support themselves in the harsh desert habitat because they will eat almost anything: from thorny cactus to tasty wild figs, and everything in between. They are social animals, living in packs of from 30 to 200 animals. Predators like coyotes and bobcats are wary of them, for they can use their tusks well, and once aroused, the whole pack will attack stubbornly. There are stories of hunters and photographers who were treed for considerable periods of time by an angry pack of peccaries, which failed to retreat even after several animals had been shot.

10

The Wolverine
(*Gulo gulo*)

The wolverine is not a large animal. Nor is it strange and disturbing in appearance. So, at first thought, it is hard to understand why it has acquired such a bad reputation. And yet, from early Indian legends down to modern trappers in the polar countries, it has been called such names as Demon, Glutton, the Evil One.

Ferris Weddle, one expert on the wolverine, quotes a trapper as saying, "I say without equivocation that the only good wolverine is a dead one. This vicious, bloodthirsty, overgrown member of the weasel family has no place in existence."

We have heard words like this before. The charge of the only good one being a dead one is still applied to the coyote, and it was used about the American Indians when white men were trying to steal their lands. But where does the wolverine fit into this?

The wolverine is the largest member of the weasel family.

It has a long, low-slung body and powerful legs. An adult is about forty inches long and weighs from forty to fifty pounds —a small carnivore rather than a large one. Its dark-brown fur, sometimes streaked with orange, is thick and coarse, with hairs that shed moisture. This makes the pelt especially desirable for trimming the openings of parkas, which otherwise would freeze when wet. And this puts a premium on wolverine fur for both the trapper and the hunter.

The animal is well armed with sharp claws and strong digging muscles. And it has a keen nose for smelling out winter provisions. Many a trapper has returned from checking his trapline to find that his supplies have been broken into by a hungry wolverine.

A wolverine

Like all members of the weasel family, the wolverine has a set of scent glands that give off a strong musky odor. And like many other predators, it has a habit of marking its food and territory to warn off other animals. So if a wolverine does not eat the looted food supply on the spot, or carry it away, it will most likely spray it with its scent, thus making it unusable for the trapper. It is this habit that has especially enraged the men who have met with it. For with his winter supplies ruined, a trapper will have to give up and return to civilization or face the possibility of starvation.

However, men who have studied the wolverine without the motive of personal profit have never failed to be impressed by this animal. Ernest Thompson Seton, one of America's great naturalists, wrote in *The Lives of Game Animals,* "The wolverine is a tremendous character . . . a personality of unmeasured force, courage, and achievement, but so enveloped in mists of legend, superstition, idolatry, fear and hatred, that one scarcely knows how to begin or what to accept as fact."

Today the mists and the legends are being cleared away by scientists who observe with an open mind. It is found that the wolverine is an animal with great energy and courage, two qualities that should be admirable in any creature. They can climb trees quickly and easily. And while they are not as swift as the wolf in pursuing game, they are persistent and tireless, and in winter their large paws act as snowshoes to give them an added advantage.

Perhaps the most remarkable thing about the wolverine is its ability to stand up to animals several times its size. A wolverine weighing forty or fifty pounds will not hesitate to attack a bear weighing hundreds of pounds. Even wolves have been known to back off from a battle with a wolverine. It has been suggested that perhaps the wolves were not very hungry and that most wild animals prefer to avoid an all-out fight when possible. Still, the wolverine presents a startling array of weapons to an enemy: long, strong claws; sharp teeth bared in powerful, snarling jaws. And above all, it launches a wild, scrappy attack, prepared to stop at nothing, which makes this medium-sized animal appear to be several times its size in menace.

This same boundless energy, the ability to leap into and out of trees, to swim rivers and hustle through dense, rough terrain, has made it possible for the wolverine to pull down prey that is many times its size. Reindeer and even elk are sometimes killed, although the victims are usually sick or old animals, or else the very young.

They also eat a variety of small game, lemmings, and other rodents; fish, frogs, and insects; birds when they can catch them, and their eggs; and during the summer, berries of all kinds. The wolverine has a big sweet tooth and is really omnivorous.

When confronted with humans, the wolverine becomes cautious. But it does not leave the neighborhood, as would a bear, lynx, or deer. It exploits the works of man. It will follow a trapline and dine off the trapped victims before the frustrated trapper can collect the pelts. And it prefers to follow a domestic herd of reindeer rather than a wild one, since the deer are kept together by the herders and are easier to catch. Of course, this leads it to kill other domestic animals, such as cattle and sheep, and adds to its bad name. But it is not easy to hunt down a wolverine. They are extremely wary and intelligent, can cover sixty miles in a day over very rough country, and don't stay around to be hunted.

All these things have made the wolverine seem almost supernatural to northern peoples. It is said to be in league with the devil, and most men living in its territory hate and shun it and believe nothing good of it.

And yet, Peter Krott, who made a two-year study of these animals in the 1950's, found them to be delightful, loving, and devoted creatures. His animals were pups, captured in the wild, which he reared from babyhood. His investigations were supported by the Swedish government, which gave him the use of a forester's lodge in one of its wild preserves.

Krott's animals all loved him and romped with his children. They were playful as puppies and went walking with him like a dog. He tells several remarkable stories of the behavior of his wolverines.

In one instance, Krott and his wife had taken their small baby, along with the wolverine, to an island in a lake, where they spent an agreeable afternoon in the woods. At one point, they left the baby asleep on its blanket while they wandered farther afield. Looking back, they saw the wolverine racing toward the sleeping child, and in spite of their experience with the animals, they were alarmed. Krott cautioned his wife not to shout or frighten the animal, and they approached at a normal walk. When they reached their baby, the wolverine was standing over it, licking its face—so gently that the child did not awake.

In another instance, Krott felt that he owed his life to one of his animals. He had taken this wolverine, a young one, on an overnight trek through the Swedish forest, and stopped for the night in a camper's hut. It was winter, and he built a good fire in the fireplace to last through the night. During the night, he was awakened by the wolverine outside. It was making a great noise, scratching at the door and running across the roof. Krott was very groggy, and when he staggered awake, he found the hut was full of smoke and that he was on the verge of suffocation. Just then the wolverine managed to push in the door, and Krott rushed out into the fresh air. Later he was undecided about the animal's motives. Had he been trying to force an entrance to escape from another wild wolverine that had been threatening him? Or was he attracted by the smell of the burning wood? Or did he realize the danger and was he trying to rescue his beloved master? Whatever the answer, the scientist was convinced that the animal had saved his life.

One characteristic of the wolverine, especially exasperating to northern woodsmen, is its habit of stealing. Food, tools, clothing, anything that can come loose, will be lifted by this wilderness thief, and campers in wolverine country go to great lengths to secure their belongings. Krott had ample opportunity to observe this trait, but having a good sense of humor, he reports his experiences as amusing incidents. He says that the males especially love to make off with anything that strikes their fancy, and Krott had to keep a careful eye on all his belongings.

In this, the wolverine resembles the crow, the jay, and the pack rat, all creatures that love to steal and hoard any interesting item they can find. Young wolverines are especially exuberant and mischievous, and Krott describes one picnic on which he took two of these young animals to an island. The pups were continually dashing from one interesting point to another. They got into the rucksack of supplies, until Krott hung it up in a tree. Then the two rascals dashed down to the water for a swim. After that they chased a squirrel up a tree and ended in a free-for-all between themselves, in which they both rolled down to the water again. After this, the male wolverine discovered the metal baling bowl that Krott kept in his boat. The pup went off with it and led Krott a merry chase. He would put it down and pretend to lose interest in it. But then, at the last second, he would snatch it away before the man's fingers could close on the rim. While this was going on, the female wolverine was climbing the tree where the rucksack was hanging, and Krott had to rush back to rescue the rations. It was all good fun—but hardly a restful picnic!

It is sad to report that these experiments resulted in the deaths of all the wolverines. They are unsocial animals when they grow up. Each adult animal has its territory, which it marks with its scent spray and defends against all others of the same sex. Thus, a wild wolverine living near Krott's dwelling tried to evict all his male animals. He would tolerate the

A wolverine

females. But females, in turn, must stay clear of the territories of other females.

This habit forced the young wolverines to move away from the preserve and into unprotected areas. And as soon as the local farmers and hunters found their tracks, the hunt was on!

Wolverines inhabit a wide territory around the polar regions, especially in the pine forests of Europe and America. This includes Alaska, Canada, Russia, and Scandinavia. As civilization encroaches on these lands, the wolverine is forced farther back into the white wilderness. Until now, he has been able to hold his own, with his quick brain, his vast energy, and his ability to put many miles between himself and pursuers.

But now a new menace has appeared: the snowmobile. With this method of transport, men can easily follow and catch up with the wolverine. And unless it is given legal protection, it will soon be drastically reduced in numbers. By the time the mists of hatred and prejudice have been cleared away, this unusual animal may have passed into oblivion.

11

The Puma

(Felis concolor)

Is it sound economy to pay out $494,000 a year for the purpose of killing wild animals that cause only $120,000 yearly damage? That is what our Fish and Wildlife Service has been doing with its predator-control program. Pumas, bears, and coyotes are the main targets, but when poison is used, many other animals fall victim also.

Some western states are beginning to rebel at this. They feel that it would be better and cheaper to pay damages to ranchers who have lost stock to wild animals, rather than to keep on contributing thousands of dollars to this predator-control program.

The puma was once the most feared and hated predator in this country. And this is understandable, for it has had the widest range. It used to live in all the forty-eight states, from the Atlantic to the Pacific. And even now it has a north-south range from Canada to Patagonia on the tip of South America. In the

centuries before Columbus, the Indians recognized the power
and beauty of this animal. Some tribes even worshiped it, and
the word "puma," in the language of the Incas, means courage
and power.

When the white men came, bringing cattle to replace the
deer and the buffalo, they soon learned to fear the puma, which
they believed was a threat to their herds. A general effort was
made to destroy the species, and as civilization moved westward,
the puma was pushed back to the mountain wilderness of the
Rockies. Until very recently, these animals were considered
varmints, and a bounty was paid for killing them by most western states.

The puma, also known as the mountain lion, the cougar, and
a number of other names, is one of the most difficult predators
to hunt and kill. It usually stays as far away as possible from
man and his dwellings, and a hunter must trail it for days before
catching sight of it. The animal travels widely over a roughly
circular range, which experts insist can be as great as 200 miles.
Thus it never stays long in one place, but can return periodically
as it retravels its route.

The male puma averages 150 pounds, and the female, 100
pounds, but there are records of even larger cats. Theodore
Roosevelt shot one in Colorado weighing 227 pounds. The
southern pumas, from Arizona, New Mexico, and Central America are usually smaller than those living farther north. The
Florida animals, which hide in the Everglades, are of a reddish
color, and the rare Louisiana cat has a dark stripe down its back.
But most mountain lions are grayish or tawny colored.

Unlike many of the cat family, the puma's eyes are round instead of oblique. These cats are fast, strong, and agile and climb
trees readily. They can make their way over the roughest
ground that would impede most other animals, leaping from
rock to rock or bounding up an almost vertical cliff.

The puma's litter may number anywhere from one to six
cubs, which are darker than the adults and spotted and whose

A puma

tails are ringed. They lose these markings as they grow older. The mother alone has charge of the rearing. She brings food to them until they are old enough to follow her on the hunt. Until they are about two years old, she trains them in the ways of the wild, teaching them all they need to know about hunting and how to protect themselves. After that, they are on their own and must face the dangers of life alone.

Since earliest times there have been records of people, especially children, being attacked by pumas. But these are exceptional cases. There are more people killed each year by deer in the United States than by pumas. As with the lion in Africa, such attacks are usually made by old or sick individuals, which can no longer catch their natural prey and are on the verge of starvation.

Normally, the puma is a shy, wary animal and hides itself from man. Perhaps it is this very furtiveness, this ability to move silently through the wilds and close in on an unsuspecting hiker, that has made it an object of fear and aversion. Of course, the puma is a powerful wild beast, and as such is to be treated with respect and caution. If cornered, especially with cubs, it will defend itself. But if there is a way out from a confrontation with man, it will quickly take it.

There are stories of pumas following hunters and circling their campfires, apparently out of curiosity. Young animals, captured in the wild and raised as pets, are friendly and playful while cubs. And the Cheyenne Indians sometimes caught such cubs and later trained them to stalk deer for the tribe.

Since colonial times the white man has set a bounty on these great animals, so that it looked as though they might disappear entirely from the American scene. When it reached the point that there were only an estimated 600 pumas still living in the state of California, conservationists in that state put up a big fight to save it. First the bounty was removed, and then the puma was declared a game animal. This meant that it could be hunted only during open seasons. However, the open season was usually four months long, giving hunters plenty of time to reduce the cat population. So the people who love true wilderness and want to keep it that way made another great effort, and in 1972 the puma was declared a Protected Mammal—for four years. The people of California hope to keep it on that list. It would be nice if other western states would follow this lead, for mountain lions do not understand state lines or park boundaries.

Until very recently, little was known about how the puma lives. There were plenty of tall tales about it, but also great disagreement among the experts. Some hunters said it screamed like a dying woman. Others said it made no noise at all. Some said it was a solitary animal and that the female alone reared the cubs. Others reported seeing the male in the family group. Some called it an agent of the devil, and others insisted that it was a beautiful animal, a part of nature.

As more and more people come to realize that predators are an important element of the wild, there is a growing demand for their protection. It is now generally accepted that you cannot have a healthy deer population without the predators that normally keep the herds down to reasonable numbers. Otherwise, the deer will eat up all their food and will starve. Control of the deer by hunting is not the same thing, for the hunters shoot the strongest and healthiest animals. The wild predators can catch only the old, the sick, and the weak. So you can see that with hunting as a population control, the herds will get weaker instead of stronger.

In this way, pumas also help to save our forests. When an area is burned off, nature has ways of replenishing it. There are certain seed cones that only open and drop their seeds when exposed to the extreme heat of a forest fire. These operate to start a new growth as soon as the ashes have cooled. Also, fireweeds and grasses, which grow quickly, move into the sunny places and start a new basic growth to hold and build the soil. However, if there is an uncontrolled deer population living in the area, they will eat up the grass and the new trees faster than they can grow. These deer will leave no plants to hold the soil in place, and soon there will be nothing but rocky, barren ground. A few mountain lions in the region can reverse this trend.

Contrary to some opinions, pumas do not kill wantonly. They save what they do not immediately eat of a kill and often hide it, covering it with sticks and leaves or scratching dirt over it. They may stay in the vicinity until they have eaten the whole carcass, perhaps for several days.

As men began to realize how much good the puma can do and that the black picture which had been built up around it was not a true one, it became evident that more facts were needed, and that the animal should be studied scientifically in order to clear away the mists and the mysteries. Such a study was begun in 1964 by Dr. Maurice G. Hornocker, a scientist at the University of Idaho. It is well that Dr. Hornocker is a tough outdoorsman, for he and his assistant tramped over 6,000 miles, often on snowshoes in the dead of winter. The snow made it easier for them to keep track of the animals they were studying.

The work was done in the Big Creek section of Idaho, a wild and primitive area of about 200 square miles, seldom invaded by men. Supplies had to be flown in, and were distributed among a half-dozen campsites dotted about the region. And Dr. Hornocker has spent many winters trailing the pumas, catching them and marking them and even wiring them for radio contact.

The traditional method of hunting pumas is with dogs. They cannot be studied from behind a blind, as some animals can, because they don't stay in one spot. They are always on the move, and wander over a wide area. Hunters trail the animals with several dogs especially trained to hunt mountain lions. The puma could easily kill one or even two dogs. But a pack of baying hounds puts it to flight. When pursued by these yapping dogs, they quickly climb a tree. The puma looks on a tree as a safe refuge. It hopes the dogs will get tired and go away. But then the hunter catches up, brings out his gun, and shoots the lion out of the tree.

Dr. Hornocker, of course, did not want to kill his pumas. He shot them with drugged darts. And here he had a problem. It was impossible to use a really immobilizing anesthetic, as with other animals, that would put the beast to sleep. The lions, in that case, would fall out of the trees and hurt themselves. So Dr. Hornocker developed a suitable tranquilizer dosage. Although the animal remained conscious, it was so groggy that it could be picked up, weighed, measured, and marked with a variety of tags and tattoos. However, this required keen judgment on the part of the scientist. He had to be sure the tranquilizer was in effect before he began to work on the animal.

Often Dr. Hornocker had to climb the tree after the puma, fasten a rope to its hind leg, and lower it gently to the ground— all while the animal was staring him in the face! On one occasion, the lion was not yet thoroughly tranquilized, and came down the tree as Dr. Hornocker was going up. It took refuge in a cave halfway up a cliff. The scientist pulled her out (groggy by this time), did all his measuring and marking, and then led her back into the cave, where she was left to sleep off the drug.

In the years spent on this study, Dr. Hornocker has made 155 captures. But this covered only 46 animals. Many of them were caught several times. One lion was caught as many as nine times. All this added facts to the study, and myths about the mountain lion began to fall right and left.

For one thing, these animals did not wander as widely as had been believed. But possibly that was because the study was made in the winter with heavy snow on the ground. Instead of the expected ranges of from 40 to 200 miles, these pumas covered from 5 to 25 square miles if they were females, and from 15 to 30 square miles if they were males.

The scientist noted that females would sometimes share a territory, but that males never did. If the territories of two males happened to overlap, the two were never in the same area at the same time. Pumas mark out their territories much as wolves

A puma

do, by scraping up a little pile of sticks and pine needles and urinating on them. These little mounds are signals to other lions to stay away, and the lions recognize and respect them. Dr. Hornocker calls this "mutual avoidance." He believes that it helps the species to survive, for it prevents fighting. In the case of solitary animals like these, if they were injured in frequent battles, there would be no pack to help them and bring food (as with wolves) and they would soon starve. It may also be a self-control on their own population, for the large territory tends to separate individuals.

Dr. Hornocker believes that while the puma is important in regulating the deer herds, it is still more important in dispersing them. In the winter deer are apt to bunch up in what are called deer yards. There they stay in a small space, where they keep the snow trodden down, and they eat up every bit of vegetation within reach. When a puma leaps into their midst, the deer flee in all directions. And while this may be hard on the deer at the moment, it serves to disperse them into smaller groups, where they are less destructive to the forest growth.

The old argument about whether the puma is silent or noisy was partly settled by Dr. Hornocker when he was given two puma kittens by the Division of Wildlife Services. Mrs. Hornocker and the children helped to rear the babies, and the scientist learned much from observing them. He says that as they grew older they began using a whistling sound when they greeted him. He found that a warbling note meant "hello"; a sharp, piercing one was an alarm; and short, intense calls said "come here."

Since studying the cubs, the scientist has heard and recognized these sounds in the wild and believes that the mountain lions communicate in this manner. This explains how pairs or groups of lions hunting together can go different ways and then come together again at a distant spot as though it had all been prearranged.

The mountain lion is a beautiful, intelligent, and useful animal. And it is greatly misunderstood. Work like Dr. Hornocker's pioneering study may clear up some of the misunderstandings and help us save this animal for future generations to marvel at and enjoy.

12

The Spotted Hyena
(*Crocuta crocuta*)

Scavengers are useful animals. In fact, they are indispensable. Dr. George B. Schaller, in his book *The Year of the Gorilla*, tells how some disease attacked the duikers—a species of African antelopes—in the area where he was working. This was at an elevation of 10,000 feet, where there were few scavengers, and he was continually coming upon dead animals in the forest. A depressing and unhygienic situation.

Because scavengers feed on dead animals (including humans, if given the chance), they are a reminder of death, and as such are considered evil, loathesome, and bringers of misfortune. People do not stop to think that they are doing a very important job in the scheme of things.

The spotted hyena is a scavenger of the African plains. It is found in most of Africa south of the Sahara. There is also a somewhat smaller hyena, the striped hyena, which inhabits southern Asia and the eastern parts of Africa. Hyenas look

A spotted hyena

quite doglike. Their footprints resemble a dog's. But scientists consider them more closely related to the cat family, and they are put in a category of their own, called the Hyaenidae.

One uncatlike feature is the hyena's feet, which, like a dog's, are built for running. Their hindquarters look weak and slope off to the rear. Nevertheless, hyenas can run as fast as 40 miles an hour when chasing a zebra or wildebeest. Another unusual characteristic is their extremely powerful jaws, which can grind up even elephant bones. A group of hyenas can demolish a carcass in a very short time, so that nothing at all is left.

It is said that in some African villages the people encourage the hyenas to act as garbage collectors. Holes are left purposely in the village walls through which the animals enter at night to devour the garbage outside the huts. In Harar, Ethiopia's ancient walled city, hyenas are even hand-fed in an effort to keep the "garbage collectors" tame. But in such places, parents are careful to keep their children in the house after dark!

The cry of the hyena has a weird and frightening quality. It has been described as a low whoop, a mad, gurgling laugh, a moaning howl. Africans have many superstitions about hyenas, and their fearsome tales have been passed on to Europeans. A strange thing about these animals is that their external sex organs appear very similar in both the males and the females. This has led to the belief that the hyena can change its sex, and stories used to be common of captive males that suddenly produced litters. However, scientists now know that the captor did not look closely enough in the beginning.

Hyenas used to be described as smelly, gruesome, cowardly animals that followed the lion at a distance and cleaned up anything that was left when the king of beasts was done eating. But with the advent of modern methods of studying animal behavior in the wilds, this picture has been discredited and many interesting facts have been brought to light, which reverse the old reputation of the mean and cowardly hyena.

The man who made the first detailed study of the hyena was Dr. Hans Kruuk, a Dutch zoologist, who spent a lot of time in Tanzania observing the animals. On moonlit nights he followed the hunting hyenas in a jeep and soon found that many of the accepted ideas about their way of life are false. Hyenas, he says, are not solitary animals, as believed, but are gregarious. And they are only scavengers on occasion. They are expert hunters. And instead of the hyena following the lion to feed off its kill, the situation is often reversed, and the lion chases the hyenas away from the meat that is rightfully theirs. Hyenas are inclined to be scavengers by day and hunters by night.

On one of the first hunts he observed, Dr. Kruuk watched a group of hyenas run down and kill an adult zebra. This was contrary to all popular notions about hyenas, but as the scientist sat in his car watching the animals feed, a still more unheard of event occurred. A lioness came out of the night and took over the carcass. At first the hyenas ran off, but then one by one they crept back. Soon the lioness was surrounded by watching hyenas, and one of these suddenly jumped forward and bit her on the rump. She whirled and struck out at it, but missed. And then another hyena made a quick rush and a bite. To the scientist's amazement, the lioness was chased off the hyenas' kill and disappeared into the bush. The hyenas went back to feeding, but not for long. Presently, two big male lions appeared, and when they trotted up to the kill, the hyenas gave way. But they didn't leave. They lay down in the grass and waited for the lions to finish their meal.

Dr. Kruuk watched this amazing performance until dawn, and just as he was leaving, a busload of tourists arrived. It stopped while everyone took pictures from the windows, and he heard one lady remark about the hyenas, "Look at them— they're waiting for the spoils!" None of the tourists imagined that the kill really belonged to the hyenas.

Among the mammals, the male is almost always larger than the female and is the boss. In this, the hyena is divergent, for the females are bigger than the males. They are gregarious animals, with a social order similar to the wolves. But it is a matriarchal society. The dominant female is top animal in the group.

Dr. Kruuk studied these groups extensively and in order to be able to recognize individual animals, he shot fifty hyenas with a dart gun, thus anesthetizing them so that he could cut distinguishing notches in their ears. Hyenas usually carry their ears perked up, and it was easy for the scientist, using binoculars, to recognize the marked beasts.

He then discovered that hyenas live in groups, and he called these groups clans. His work was done in the Serengeti National Park and the Ngorongoro Crater. It was easier to study the clans in the crater because there the great herds of grazing animals, and the predators that feed on them, do not migrate, but live a fairly settled life within the walls of the huge crater.

Dr. Kruuk found that there were eight hyena clans within the crater and that they had divided the region among themselves, with boundaries which they marked by leaving scent markers along the edge. Any animal that ventured into another territory was in danger of being attacked and mauled or even killed if found by members of the other clan.

The center of clan life is the den with the young. The females of a clan make their dens close together in a community, and often the pups are moved from den to den for one reason or another. Males are kept at a distance when there are babies in the dens, and Dr. Kruuk learned the reason in a dramatic incident.

He had been given a baby hyena that one of the rangers had found, and he and his wife bottle-fed it, for they believed that by having a pet hyena they could learn more about the animals. Solomon, as the hyena was called, quickly won their hearts. But one night they were awakened by hearing the young hyena scream outside their cabin. Kruuk rushed outside with a flashlight and saw an adult hyena carrying off his pet. By waving his light and yelling, he made the marauder drop its prey. But poor little Solomon had a broken jaw, a torn throat, and a pierced windpipe. With the help of penicillin, he was pulled through. And Dr. Kruuk had learned one more thing about hyenas. They can on occasion be cannibals.

Another devoted observer of hyenas is Baroness Jane van Lawick-Goodall. With her husband, Hugo, a wildlife photographer, she is the author of that excellent book *Innocent Killers*. She, too, operated from a car—a station wagon that she parked close by the community den at a place called Scratching Rocks. (It is the zebras, not the hyenas, that scratch themselves against the rocks.) Often her young son, Grublin, slept in the back of the car while she took notes on the home life of the hyenas.

Jane did not find it necessary to mark her hyenas. Close observation soon made it possible for her to distinguish many of the sixty individuals of the Scratching Rocks clan. The dominant female was a battle-scarred individual, whom Jane called Bloody Mary. She was blind in one eye, but she still retained her authority over all the other hyenas in the clan. It was she who led in a chase after zebra or in a battle with another clan of hyenas. At such times her tail was curled up over her back, her shoulder hair bristled, and she rushed into the fray uttering all the frightful sounds of which a hyena is capable.

Bloody Mary had a close friend, another female, whom Jane called Lady Astor. The two were often seen together. They hunted and fought their enemies together. They wallowed in the mud together. And they denned close to each other, and their pups all played together. Jane suspected that they were sisters, but there was no way she could be sure.

Other, lower-ranking hyena females denned in the same community, and hyena society seems to be built around these family groups. When a member arrives at the dens, he or she goes through an elaborate greeting ritual with the hyenas already there. They smell and lick each other's mouths and also around the hind legs. This is similar to the greeting pattern used by dogs and other canines. Even the very young greet the arriving adults and also each other as they move from den to den. Sometimes a mother, returning from a hunt with a bone for her youngster, will have to look through several dens before she finds him.

Most mammals wean their young after a few weeks, but hyena cubs go on suckling until well into their second year. Often the mother is still trying to wean the youngster when it is a year and a half old and almost as big as she is. The reason seems to be that hyenas do not bring home meat from a kill— a bone for a plaything is as close as they get—nor do they re-gurgitate food at the den, as many of the canines do.

A hyena kill is a rough and violent affair. It requires running long distances, often after an animal that may turn and charge with horns down or bite as zebras do. Hyenas prefer to attack from the rear and en masse. But even so, they can be injured. The scientists tell of watching some thirty hyenas chasing a herd of 200 zebras. They were in a bunch behind one fleeing animal, and the observers saw a hyena kicked into the air by the zebra's hooves. It rolled over twice when it hit the ground, but then picked itself up and went on running.

Hunted animals sometimes try to escape by running into water, but hyenas are good swimmers and not afraid to dash in after them. In fact, they have been seen to dive into deep water after a drowned beast and even pull it ashore.

Once the prey is brought down, there is a free-for-all among the hyenas, each one trying to get its share, with no holds barred. Hyenas are often bitten by their clanmates in these scrimmages. One female that Jane found easy to recognize had lost the whole tip of her nose—probably in one of these battles for food. In addition, the kill may be usurped by lions. And there are usually other thieves to contend with, such as jackals and vultures. It is not a safe place for a young cub, until he learns how to hold his own.

So hyena cubs are nursed for a long time, and this makes the mother-child relationship much stronger than in some animals. Jane tells of watching Lady Astor nurse her daughter, who was almost as big as she was. As the big cub nestled up to her, the mother laid a paw across its flank in a gesture of love and companionship. However, not so long after this, the scientist watched the efforts of the mother to wean her cub and the tantrum that the young hyena indulged in. The mother often had to nip the youngster to make her desist in her efforts, and the cub would then squeal loudly and rush after her mother, only to be nipped again. This behavior often degenerated into a scrap between mother and daughter, which was repeated daily.

Hyenas are very playful animals, but as this behavior takes

place at night, it is no wonder that playfulness is not part of the popular myth. On many a moonlit night Jane watched a group of cubs, from several mothers and of varying ages, climb all over Bloody Mary, the otherwise dignified and aggressive leader of the Scratching Rocks clan. Several youngsters would be pulling at her ears while another bit her tail and still others attacked her middle. Finally, the female hyena would heave herself up, scattering cubs in every direction, and would start to run in a wide circle. The cubs would dash after her, each trying to get a tooth-hold on her tantalizing tail.

Male hyenas are not as closely bound to the central core of the clan. They wander about, occasionally stopping by the dens to greet the females and their offspring. But they are chased away if there are very small cubs around. To her surprise, Jane discovered that some males occasionally move from one clan to another. Female hyenas guard their territories with great ferocity, going on regular boundary-marking trips in which each animal follows the example of the leader in depositing a scent marker on certain rocks or bits of vegetation. Hyenas try to push back their boundaries and enlarge their territories if they can, but if the neighboring clan discovers this—as when a kill has been made just over the border—they will assert their rights with vigor, and a number may be killed or badly hurt in the ensuing brawl.

So the scientist watched with great interest the actions of a young male that she called Quiz. This animal was about four years old and held high rank in the Scratching Rocks clan. He even lorded it over a few of the females. So it was doubly surprising to find him making friends with members of the neighboring Lakeside clan. The incident occurred when the Scratching Rocks hyenas had made a kill near the border. While they were feeding, the Lakeside clan assembled on the boundary and stood there, growling and whooping, trying to get up the courage to cross the border and dispute the kill. Then two big lions turned up and took the kill away from the rightful owners.

Jane now had the interesting picture of two hyena clans lined up on opposite sides of their boundary, walking up and down aggressively and watching the lions eat their food. Suddenly, a single hyena walked out into the space between the two clans. This was Quiz. He approached the Lakeside clan and stood with his head up and his tail down, and presently another hyena came from the Lakeside clan and joined him and they went through some of the hyena greeting rituals. But then Quiz looked up and saw eight Lakeside hyenas bearing down on him with their tails curled up aggressively, and he turned and ran back to his own clan. He ran right up to Bloody Mary and began the greeting rituals, rubbing and nosing and licking around her mouth and legs, crouching down and wagging his tail. He repeated this with other members of the clan, seeming to ask their pardon for making friends with the Lakeside clan.

Jane thought this would put an end to the fraternization, but twenty minutes later, when most of the Lakeside clan had departed, she saw Quiz go back across the line and start friendly overtures with the five remaining animals. Later, when the lions had gone away, the Scratching Rocks hyenas moved up to feed. They would not let the five Lakesiders join them, and Quiz remained aloof, lying down with his new friends to watch his clan eat. It was a back-and-forth proposition, with Quiz sometimes going to feed with his clan and then going back to fraternize with the Lakesiders. But when he dared to put his own scent mark on the Lakesiders' marking place, it was too much for his new friends, and they chased him back to his own territory. On other occasions, Hugo twice saw Quiz feeding with the Lakeside clan at their kills.

Jane was especially interested in the hyena's courting behavior, but she never saw it culminate in the mating act. The courting ritual is a kind of bowing indulged in by the male. Watching Lady Astor when she was in heat, Jane saw one of the lower-status males approach. The female was lying in the grass and paid no attention to her suitor, who bowed until his head was almost on the ground and then made quick digging motions with his paw. He kept this up until he was almost on top of Lady Astor, when she raised her head and looked at him. He turned tail and ran so fast that he fell over a clump of grass. This behavior was repeated for two hours, when it became dark. At that point, Lady Astor got up and walked into the nearby bed of reeds, with her suitor at her heels. Unfortunately, the station wagon could not be driven into the reed bed.

The next day, and for six days following, Lady Astor was courted in the same manner, each day by a different male, each one slightly higher on the status scale. Finally, the top male (whom Jane called Wellington) took over and drove off all the other male hyenas. He, too, went through the same bowing and digging ritual, once even digging at Lady Astor's back. And while he hastily retreated after this rash action, she did not bite at him. In the end, as with all the others, Lady Astor got up and wandered into the reeds with Wellington close behind, and the scientist was left to imagine the conclusion.

Hyenas are powerful animals, the female weighing as much as 130 pounds. They are the most numerous predators on the African plains, and while they produce only one or two young to a litter, as opposed to the four to six of other species, they are very successful in the fight for survival. To achieve this, they have had to battle every step of the way, not only in the chase to pull down their prey, but also in the struggle to keep and eat it when the bigger and stronger lions try to take it away. Or when other hyenas, as well as jackals and buzzards, try to cut in.

Hyenas can be dangerous, too. They have been known to carry off children and to attack sleeping people. But they are less apt to attack a person who stands still and faces them. Their instinct is to chase what runs away, and if a man stands still, they are in doubt about the quarry. This behavior can be seen also in dogs.

More than any animal, the hyena reminds me of the human species, which has arrived at the top of the survival heap by constant aggression, against its own kind as well as against other species. But like us, the hyena has a softer, loving side. The bond between the females and the young is very strong, as is that between siblings. One sad story in the Van Lawick-Goodalls' book concerns Bloody Mary's two pups, which Jane called Vodka and Cocktail. They were twins, and since it is impossible to tell the sex of hyenas until they become adult, she accepted them both as males. However, there was a great difference in their characters. Vodka was bold and Cocktail was shy. Vodka took to going on hunts at an early age, squirming under Bloody Mary's legs to get at the kill. But Cocktail stayed at home. For this reason, Jane began to think that Vodka might be a female.

One morning the scientist parked her car by the dens and found Bloody Mary lying outside with Vodka. But the youngster was restless. He (she?) kept sniffing around, looking across the plains. He looked inside the den. Then he ran off to a neighboring den, with Bloody Mary following. He looked in there. Jane, in her car, followed the two from den to den in their fruitless search. Often the young hyena dug out the dens as though that action might produce his sibling. The mother followed along, not seeming alarmed. But by evening, when no Cocktail had appeared, she took up the search, going from den to den and calling softly into each. She continued this for two days, mourning softly as she poked her nose down each hole.

Jane never saw Cocktail again. The young hyena was just one more casualty of the African wild.

13

The Indian Dhole
(Cuon alpinus)

When Rudyard Kipling, the famous British author of the nine-teenth century, was writing his children's classic *The Jungle Book,* he needed a villain for his Indian Eden. After all, he could not make all the animals the noble friends of little Mowgli and have any excitement or menace in his stories. So while the wolves, the bear, the panther, the elephant, and even the snake were all "good guys," who helped Mowgli to adjust to jungle living, the tiger was painted as a villain, who had wanted to eat Mowgli when he was a baby, and continued with that purpose throughout the book.

Now we all know that a wolf or a panther or even a bear might be just as apt to eat a baby, if given the chance, as a tiger. But Kipling's stories are so charmingly told that we accept the essential goodness of all the animals except the tiger. Still, one tiger was hardly enough to keep the action moving, so Kipling wrote a chapter called "Red Dog," in which he introduced the Asiatic wild dog, or dhole.

Here is how he describes the animals: "They drive straight through the jungle, and what they meet they pull down and tear to pieces. Though they are not as big nor half as cunning as the wolf, they are very strong and very numerous. The dhole, for instance, do not begin to call themselves a pack till they are a hundred strong, whereas forty wolves make a very fair pack." And again, "A little before midday when the sun was very warm, he heard the patter of feet and smelt the abominable smell of the dhole pack as they trotted steadily and pitilessly along Wontolla's trail." And later on, "The brute looked up and his companions halted behind him, scores and scores of red dogs with low-hung tails, heavy shoulders, weak quarters, and bloody mouths."

How accurate is this description today? Most observers, writing in such publications as the *Journal of the Bombay Natural History Society,* complain that the wild dogs are ruthless and wanton killers and that they soon scare away or kill off all the game in an area where they are hunting. But these accounts smack too much of the hunter who wants to hold onto top-priority rights to the game. In one instance, the writer had gone to hunt bear and told how the only way to chase the bears out of their caves was to throw a bomb into the opening. While the hunters were at this game, they heard a disturbance upstream. They investigated, and found a group of wild dogs attacking three deer. They fired at the dogs and chased them away, congratulating themselves on having saved the deer from a horrible death. But who would rescue the bears from the hunters' bombs? These men never considered that the wild dog, like all living creatures, must eat, and cannot go home to a nice meal of roast mutton at the end of a day of sport.

The Indian wild dog is a canine weighing about forty pounds. It is smaller than a wolf, has a shorter muzzle and rounder ears. It also has fewer molars in the lower jaw and

Wild dogs attacking a deer

more nipples: six or seven pairs instead of the usual canine five. In color, they are reddish-brown with coarse hair. The dogs found in Java, Sumatra, and Malaya are brighter colored than those native to India.

Like all the canines, these wild dogs are built for running. Wolves and other members of the dog family run on their toes. And in this process of running down their prey, they have lost the use of the fifth toe, which now appears, if it does so at all, as a dewclaw. This is in contrast to their cousins, the bears, which walk flat-footed, have kept all their toes, and do not try to catch their prey by chasing it.

The dhole is described as a relentless runner, which seldom gives up its pursuit once it has selected its prey. As a rule, dholes hunt the smaller species of deer, the little barking deer, the musk deer, the spotted deer, or the sambar. But when such are not available, they do not hesitate to attack wild boar or large wild cattle, such as the gaur and banteng. When very hungry, they have even been known to kill a bear or a tiger. In attacking these large, dangerous animals, the whole pack works together and overcomes the victim by sheer weight of numbers. Of course, a number of wild dogs may be hurt or killed in the process.

One story is told of a Bengal tiger, which took refuge in a tree to escape a pack of dholes. The dogs laid siege to the tree, and when the tiger finally tired of his position and tried to escape by jumping down, the pack fell upon him, tore him to pieces, and ate him. How large are these packs? Kipling mentions packs of one or two hundred, but most modern reports cite five to ten dogs. Was Kipling exaggerating for effect? Or has the dhole population decreased drastically?

Any animal that can chew up a tiger is bound to get a reputation for ferocity. In the past, writers on India's wildlife have characterized this animal as the fiercest, most bloodthirsty, and most hated animal in the jungle. "Vile creatures, the terror of the wild denizens of the jungle and the enemy of the sportsman," is the description given by one early writer.

Little serious, scientific work has been done on the dhole. Most of the new wave of zoologists, studying the behavior and life habits of animals, have gone to Africa. However, there is another species of wild dog living in Africa. This is the Cape hunting dog (*Lycaon pictus*). And while it differs from the dhole in appearance, its habits and its reputation among sportsmen are remarkably similar.

Beginning in the 1960's, this African wild dog has been studied by a number of dedicated scientists, and it has been found that far from being the ravening monster that its reputation suggests, it leads an extraordinarily loving and generous home life. Dogs greet each other with every sign of love and friendship, and the pack returning from a hunt promptly regurgitates food for the female that was left at home to guard the pups. When older, the pups are fed by regurgitation. And every dog, male or female, takes part in rearing the little ones. In fact, the returning pack is so excited about getting back to the babies, licking and fondling them, that the real mother has trouble getting her pups to herself long enough to nurse them!

It seems reasonable to expect that when some scientist gets around to making a study of the dhole, it will be found that this animal has a very similar nature. For after all, the dhole is only a wild dog in the exact meaning of the words. Anyone who has owned a dog is aware of the loving trust and devotion that are the basis of the dog's nature. And where did the dog get his capacity for love? From his wild ancestors—the wolf, the jackal, perhaps the coyote, and just possibly the wild dogs. In nature, this love is directed toward the other members of the family and pack. When domesticated, it is directed toward the person who tends the animal.

But we don't need to wait for the scientific survey to get an insight into these things. Enough people have written in the pages of the *Bombay Journal,* telling of unusual experiences with wild dogs. As long ago as 1951, there was a record of a red female village dog that used to play with the wild dogs when they appeared in the neighborhood. Still another village dog— black and white this time—is said to have followed the wild dog pack. It would ingratiate itself among the dogs by lying on the ground and whining in typical canine fashion. When it returned, it was always well fed, so that the villagers took to following it, hoping to get some meat, too!

Another report comes from Joyce Winterbotham, who was walking her dogs one evening when they picked up the trail of what turned out to be a pack of dholes. One dog was a golden retriever, and as she was boarding this dog for friends, she was worried when he disappeared into the jungle. When she called, her three small black dogs quickly returned with their tails down. But it took some persistent whistling to call the retriever back. When he did appear, he was leading a pack of wild dogs, which seemed to have accepted him as one of their own!

There are also a number of instances in which wild dogs have been tamed and have made good pets. However, the writers point out that the pups must be taken from the den when they are still very young. There are usually from two to six pups in a litter and sometimes even more. One observer reports finding several dens in one place, pointing to the close social behavior of the animals.

Five such pups, raised in captivity, were nursed by a village dog until weaned. It was noted that they fought furiously among themselves until they reached a certain age, when all fighting ceased. They had apparently established their "pecking order," and knew which dog was the strongest. This one was respected and accepted as the leader, and they never fought each other after they became adult.

In another case, a man in Mysore raised two wild dogs, which became quite devoted to him. And a writer who signs himself "Robin Hood" describes his six dhole puppies as "lovely little russet-red balls of fur," and claims that for "gameness, staunchness and invincible tenacity, we have no breed of domestic dog to compare with them."

So perhaps the Indian dhole is not universally misunderstood. However, like all wild animals today, the dholes face a shrinking habitat with the encroachment of civilization upon even the wildest and most remote corners of the world. Writing in a report to the New York Zoological Society in 1971, Dr. George B. Schaller says that he found little understanding of the role of predators in India. When visiting a wildlife sanctuary there, he saw a pack of thirteen dholes feeding on a newly killed deer. The forest officer urged that all such predators be shot. But in the next breath, the man complained that there were too many deer and that it might be necessary to shoot some of them. Dr. Schaller suggested that the wild predators, like the dholes, might be a better control of overpopulation among the deer than men with guns. But the Indian did not agree.

The scientist left with the haunting thought that these interesting members of the dog family, along with the tiger and the leopard, may be wiped out by man's guns and traps and poisons before we have had time to study them and reach a true appreciation of their nature and their worth.

14

The Gorilla
(Gorilla gorilla)

Strange as it may seem, the gorilla, our closest relative among the animals, with the possible exception of the chimpanzee, has been the most viciously libeled and slandered by us in the past. Only within the last decade or two have we begun to understand the true nature of the gorilla.

One reason for this may be the fact that people have always loved scary stories about monsters and terrible, ferocious beasts. Even though most of the dangerous animals have been killed off and the stories about monsters and goblins have been refuted, we still have a lurking desire to be frightened by something bigger, stronger, or more bloodthirsty than we are.

The gorilla was the last of the great apes to be discovered. The lowland form was found and proof of its existence brought to Europe in 1847, and not until 1902 was the mountain gorilla discovered. But vague stories, myths, and writings about huge, hairy, manlike creatures go back to the ancient world.

In the fifth century B.C. a Carthaginian named Hanno sailed around the top of Africa and down the west coast. He brought back stories of a race of savage, hairy "men" found on an island in a gulf. The interpreters called them "gorillas." This is the first recorded use of the word. Hanno's men succeeded in capturing three of the hairy "women," but as they fought and bit and refused to go with the explorers, they were killed and skinned and the skins brought back to Carthage.

Scientists are still in doubt as to what Hanno found. He was probably in modern Sierra Leone, where today there are chimpanzees. Gorillas now live only far inland, but it is possible that in 500 B.C. their range was more extensive. Still, it seems more probable that Hanno's men captured chimpanzees.

From that time onward, Greek and Roman legends and later history are full of tales of great, hairy, manlike creatures, very dangerous to man and living somewhere in the far corners of the earth. By the time of the great voyages of discovery in the fifteenth and sixteenth centuries, more rumors abounded. An Englishman named Andrew Battell, who lived around 1600, visited Africa and wrote of his experiences. He may have been the first European to see both the chimpanzee and the gorilla. He tells us, "The Woods are so covered with Baboons, Monkies, Apes, and Parrots, that it will feare any man to trauaile in them alone. Here are also two kinds of Monsters, which are common in these Woods, and very dangerous." Battell called his large ape a "pongo." The word has been taken into scientific terminology to describe the apes.

In all these early accounts the ferocity of the animal is given first importance, probably because it played up the dangers confronted by the explorer and his courage in surmounting them. But along with the development of sailing went the growth of science. All new discoveries had to be brought home and given to the scientists for study. And while the chimpanzee, the orangutan, and the many New World monkeys were duly examined and given their niches in the zoological picture, no huge hominid

A lowland gorilla

turned up until the middle of the nineteenth century. By that
time, the scientists had decided that it did not exist and that the
stories were just travelers' tales and part of the old myths and
legends.

Then, in 1847, the scientific world was astonished to learn
that there really was a giant ape whose appearance lived up to
some of the most fearsome descriptions in the legends. An
American missionary who was interested in chimpanzees came

upon a giant skull and realized that it must be a new species. He managed to obtain specimens, which were then described by scientists in the journals, and the gorilla was established as a fact.

The civilized world was electrified by this discovery and there was a rush of hunters to Africa to bring back dead gorillas for museums and, if possible, live ones for zoos. Most of the hunters also brought back stories calculated to reinforce the picture of a truly terrible monster. Vernon Reynolds, in his fine book *The Apes,* says that the human response on first sighting a gorilla is so emotional that it is almost impossible for most observers to give an objective description. The great size and strength and ugliness (by our standards) are so overwhelming, and the roar and chest-beating behavior of the male gorilla are so frightening, that one's judgment is unbalanced.

One of the first men to go to Africa in search of the gorilla, and then to write about it, was Paul du Chaillu, an American trader. From 1856 to 1859 he traveled through the dark continent (as it was then called) and brought back a large collection of animals and birds. He is supposedly the first white man to have shot a full-grown male gorilla. He describes the beast's eyes as flashing fire while the crest of hair on its head rose up and down and its mouth opened to show the great fangs and to emit a thunderous roar. "And now truly he reminded me of nothing but some hellish dream creature, a being of that hideous order, half-man, half-beast . . ."

Du Chaillu was very popular with audiences in Europe and America and his book sold well. But it was later proved to be full of exaggerations and errors, and before long the critics found that a lot of his material was taken from other sources. However, it inspired many to follow his example. One young Englishman, Winwood Reade, went to Africa to look for the gorilla. Although he never saw one, he heard a group feeding near him in the jungle. He advanced cautiously, with his guides and bearers following. "I was trembling all over," he writes, "and I could feel my eyes dilating as if they would burst from my head. I grasped my gun tightly and clenched my teeth." At this point, he stepped on a dry stick, which broke with a sharp crack. "The noise ahead of us ceased for a moment. Then there was a mighty rush, followed by infernal silence. The gorilla had run away!"

Reade came back to England with an entirely different picture of the gorilla from his predecessors. However, it was not a picture to kindle the imagination of the folks at home. And stories of monstrous, evil apes have continued to be popular. The best known of these inventions are the Tarzan books of Edgar Rice Burroughs. Burroughs never went to Africa and his "apes" are far from scientific. They seem to be a kind of cross between the gorilla and the chimpanzee. But as they are pictured as being very large, vicious, and evil, people think of them as gorillas. After all, everyone can now see a gorilla in the zoo, and he certainly presents a picture of hideous, brute strength. There he sits, behind the strongest bars available, on a cement floor, far from his native jungle, without companionship, and with nothing to do but glare at his observers. A man might go insane in such a situation. But the gorilla is only an animal —a monster animal at that.

What is the true character of the gorilla? It is only when animals are observed in their natural environment, living as they are meant to live, that this question can be answered. With the beginning of the twentieth century, scientific interest in animals began to shift from the study and description of their physical form to the study of their behavior—how they live and adapt to their environment. Early in this century an American called Carl Akeley went to Africa to collect specimens for the Museum of Natural History in New York. His collection of gorillas is still there on display. But in addition to shooting for science, he came to realize the importance of studying and learning about this animal. He also feared that it might become extinct before that study could be made. It was because of his efforts and urgings that the Albert National Park was established in what was then the Belgian Congo. This covers much of the habitat of the gorilla and offers the animal some protection.

Akeley died in Africa of a fever, before he could finish the work he had envisioned. In his writings, he maintained that the gorilla is not a monster but a "perfectly amiable and decent creature." Scientists were beginning to accept this picture, but the general public preferred to be frightened by movies like *King Kong.*

It was not until almost forty years later that a serious, in-depth study of the gorilla was made. The young scientist who accomplished this was George B. Schaller. He spent two years in Africa studying the mountain gorilla. His book *The Year of the Gorilla* is now a classic and one of the most exciting and absorbing animal books ever written. Once and for all, the old myth of a "monster" is put to rest. The gorilla emerges from the pages of Schaller's book as perhaps the most peaceable animal on the face of the earth.

The first part of Schaller's stay in Africa was given over to a survey of the gorilla population in the Congo, Uganda, and Rwanda. At that time, he estimated their numbers as between 5,000 and 15,000 animals. Later the young scientist's wife joined him, and they went to live in a cabin in Albert National Park at an elevation of 10,000 feet. This was Kabara, where Carl Akeley had worked and died almost forty years earlier and where he is now buried. It is an idyllic spot, situated in a meadow and surrounded by volcanoes and by impenetrable forests. And this was the realm of the mountain gorilla.

Schaller decided early to scrap the old methods of travel and work in Africa. It had long been the custom to go on safari with a large group of natives, who carried the baggage and equipment, cooked the meals, and did all the menial work. The scientist could see that such a party of men, trekking through the forest, would quickly scare all the animals away. On his ex-ploratory trips into the wild, he used only two or three men, carrying an equal load himself. And when he and his wife went to settle at Kabara, although their supplies were carried up to their camp by fifty-five porters, these men all departed when that job was done. The Schallers hired one young native to help with such work as chopping wood and washing clothes; and a park guard stayed with them and sometimes accompanied George into the forest. Otherwise, they were alone in the wilderness.

Although they were in central Africa, almost on the equator, the climate was cold because of the high elevation. It rained a great deal of the time and when not raining was often damp and foggy. But in spite of the depressing weather, Schaller set off at once to look for the gorillas. He did not carry a gun or any weapon. His tools were binoculars, camera, and notebook. He had to work out his own methods for getting close to the animals and observing them.

At first, whenever the gorillas saw him, they ran away, usually letting out a blood-curdling yell and sometimes pausing to put on the chest-pounding display that had so alarmed the early explorers. But Schaller soon gave up any effort at trying to hide himself. He argued that if he stayed hidden from the animals, he would miss seeing a great many of their activities. So he made it a practice to stay within view, but to remain quiet and do nothing to alarm them. Soon the group under observation began to accept him as part of the scenery. In fact, they often displayed curiosity and would approach him quite closely. The scientist either stood beside a tree or sat down at its base. Sometimes he would station himself up in a tree on a favorable limb, where he could watch what went on below.

On one occasion, when he was sitting like this in a tree, watching a group of the animals, one of the gorillas noticed him and roared. Then the whole group advanced toward the tree, stopping only thirty feet away. But it was curiosity rather than annoyance that motivated them. Presently, one female came closer, reached out and tugged at the end of Schaller's branch.

When this produced no effect, she climbed up on the branch and sat next to the scientist, looking sideways at him now and then, as though trying to understand this strange phenomenon. When she climbed down, her place was taken, first by a juvenile and then by another female. After that, the gorillas all withdrew, having satisfied their curiosity, and went about their business.

Before long, he took to spending the night with the gorillas, for he wanted to watch them as they prepared for bed and made their nests, and later to record their first actions in the morning. In all his work, he was never threatened by the gorillas or felt himself in any danger.

Schaller describes the gorillas as really magnificent animals, far more handsome and healthy than those that are seen in zoos, where the hair is often rubbed off against the cement floor and the animal sits around in a state of boredom. These animals had long, thick hair that glistened in the sun. The adult males sometimes reached six feet in height and were estimated to weigh over 400 pounds. (In zoos they often reach 600 pounds, as they get no exercise to burn up the calories.)

Schaller divided his gorillas into four age categories: infants (up to three years, when they stay close to their mothers); juveniles (between three and six years); adults, male and female; and finally, the silver-backed males, which were the leaders of the groups. Between the ages of nine and ten years, the hair on the backs of the males turns silver-gray. At this age, the male has grown to his full capacity and is in a position to assert his authority as the leader of a group.

The scientist found eleven groups, which he studied as they moved in and out of the area around Kabara. In some of the groups, he felt that he learned to know the individual gorillas intimately. Groups could be as small as five animals or as large as twenty-seven. Most groups had only one silver-backed male, the leader. But two of the groups had four silver-backs and one group had two. There seemed to be no friction between the leading silver-backs and the other males, whether black-backed or silver-backed.

Gorillas are primarily vegetarian. They eat no insects or birds' eggs or other animals, although they will eat meat and eggs in captivity. They live in a lush rain forest and are closely surrounded by the food they like best. All they have to do is sit down and reach out. Unlike chimpanzees and monkeys, they do not specialize in the flowers and fruit of plants. They eat leaves and stems alike, and they do not have to climb to the tops of trees to find their food. This is just as well, as the higher branches would break with the gorilla's great weight. But although the gorilla spends most of its time on the ground, it can and does climb into the trees. The younger ones climb more readily than the adults, and often make their nests there. And some adults climb more than others.

The life of a gorilla is uneventful by our standards. They do not awaken until the sun is well up in the sky. The first order of business is to fill their stomachs, which they do by sitting in a convenient spot and reaching out to the surrounding greenery. Schaller counted twenty-nine species of plants eaten by gorillas, but the most popular were wild celery, bedstraw, and, surprisingly, thistles and nettles. These last grow tall in that climate, and caused the scientist plenty of trouble when he had to push his way through them. Often he had red welts on his legs and arms. But the gorillas ate the plants as delicacies.

When the leader of a group decides that there might be better food a bit farther along the trail, he gets up and moves. Then his group moves along with him. This process of eating and moving continues for about two hours. By then the gorillas have filled their stomachs and are ready for their noon nap. They were never seen to drink water. Apparently, the juicy plants supply all the water they need.

The siesta extends into the early afternoon, during which time the gorillas lie close to the silver-backed male or sprawl in the sun—if there *is* any sun. At this time, they may indulge in

A lowland gorilla

the grooming routine typical of all primates. They scratch themselves, parting the hair in search of dirt or insects and re-
moving anything they find. Sometimes they groom each other.
Females do this more often than males, and juveniles more often
than females. Infants are carefully groomed and cleaned by
their mothers.

At this time, the young ones play and wander about. Since
the group is not moving ahead, there is less chance of the little
ones being left behind and lost. Sometimes a group of youngsters will climb all over the huge silver-back, sitting in his lap
and sliding down his back. Mostly they are tolerated, but if they
become too rambunctious, one look is enough to send them
away.

Later in the afternoon there is more feeding, and then as

evening approaches, the leader picks a spot for the night. When he begins to make his nest, it is a signal for all the others to do likewise. Most gorilla nests are made on the ground, but sometimes the animals go into the trees to nest. Nest building seems to be instinctive, as very young animals do it, and it has been observed in a young captive gorilla. It is done by sitting down (either on the ground or on a branch) and bending the surrounding leaves and branches inward to make a circular nest or tree platform. The animal pushes the leaves down and sits or steps on them. Sometimes it breaks off additional leaves or twigs to add to the nest. Nests are used only once and then abandoned as the group moves on.

Earlier writers thought that gorilla groups defended their territories and that the dominant male forced the younger males to leave the group, thus accounting for the occasional solitary gorilla that was sighted. Schaller found that these theories were incorrect.

His gorilla groups wandered in a rather aimless way over a wide range, always returning in time to the area around Kabara, where he was working. Since a number of groups crisscrossed this area, it was inevitable that they would at times meet each other. But when such meetings took place, there was no fighting to speak of or defending of territory. Usually the two groups mingled amicably, eating and even sleeping together. Then as their directions of movement parted, the two groups would go their separate ways. Very occasionally, a member of one group would go off with the other group.

Furthermore, Schaller never saw any animal forced to leave a group. The very fact that three of the groups contained more than one silver-backed male shows the extraordinary tolerance among these beasts. The scientist did observe several solitary males, but he also noted their unusual behavior. Apparently, these males were loners because they wanted to be. They had not been expelled from the group, but periodically wandered off when they felt like it and rejoined the group at a later time.

Neither the leader nor the group took any notice of this behavior.

Schaller was able to observe only two matings, but there again the behavior was unexpected. In neither case was the silver-backed leader involved. And in one instance, the male was one of the wandering loners. In both cases, the mating took place in full view of the rest of the group, none of which paid the slightest attention.

Schaller saw several baby gorillas soon after birth. On one of his first days of gorilla-watching, he saw a female come out of the bushes carrying a baby that had just been born, for it was still wet. She went up to the huge silver-backed male, who was standing on a low mound, gazing out over the mountains. She leaned against him, and he looked at the baby, which was feebly waving its legs and arms. Then he reached over and fondled it with his huge hand.

As they grow older, infants play such games as swinging and sliding in the trees, king-of-the-castle, and follow-the-leader. They learn which leaves are good to eat by watching their mothers, and sometimes by taking food out of their mothers' mouths. Once the scientist saw a mother gorilla take a leaf away from a baby when it had picked the wrong thing. But he never saw a mother actually hand food to an infant, as chimpanzees do.

Schaller says that gorillas, like many animals, will not look another straight in the eye for any length of time. Such staring is considered a threatening action, and Schaller himself was careful to avert his gaze so as not to disturb the animals he was watching. He also refrained from prolonged use of binoculars, as these seemed like staring eyes to the gorillas. This tactful conduct was rewarded by the trust of the gorillas. As they became used to him, they grew curious and often approached him for a better view. One young male, whom he called Junior, became almost friendly, coming close to his observation post to show off, and even sleeping at the foot of his tree. He noticed that when this young gorilla approached, he often shook his head, which seemed to be a conciliatory gesture. Schaller shook his head back, and later used this gesture when he met a gorilla unexpectedly in the forest.

In case I have given the impression that there is never any violence or dissent in gorillaland, I must admit that these animals do occasionally have a short spat or disagreement. But because each animal in a group knows its place in the "pecking order," such quarrels are seldom serious. Schaller describes one meeting between two groups that was not quite as peaceful and friendly as usual. These were groups 7 and 11, the first with eighteen members and the second with sixteen. Each had but one silver-backed male.

When Schaller observed the meeting, the leader of one group sat staring at the ground, his followers gathered behind him. The other silver-backed male approached to within twenty feet and began to show off. He hooted and growled. He beat his chest and climbed up on a log, to jump forward and land with a crash, thumping the ground with his hand. The first silver-back took up the challenge and walked toward the other male until their faces were only a foot apart and they were staring into each other's eyes. Apparently, the largest and most terrifying beast of the forest settles its quarrels by trying to stare the other fellow down! When neither would give in after about thirty seconds, the first male went back to his seat. He still tried a couple of bluffs, rising up to his full height, throwing a handful of leaves into the air, and rushing at the other male, to stop with his face only an inch from the other's. But neither could out-bluff the other, and eventually they both went back to feeding. Meanwhile, the two groups of followers paid no attention and went about their regular activities. As they wandered along, they passed right under the tree where Schaller was sitting.

The scientist says that he never got used to the roar of a gorilla, even when he saw that it was coming. The shattering noise always made him want to run, but he felt some compensation in noting that the other gorillas seemed to be just as startled. Schaller discovered that this famous gorilla display actually has nine steps to it, although the complete sequence is not always given.

At first, the male sits up and hoots softly, starting slowly and going faster and faster. The hooting seems to excite him. Sometimes he stops for a moment and picks a single leaf from the nearest plant, which he puts between his lips. Just before the climax, he rises up on his hind legs, at the same time ripping some more leaves from the bushes, which he throws into the air. The climax is the famous act of beating his chest. The gorilla slaps his slightly cupped hands from two to twenty times against his chest or legs. During or right after this climax he is apt to run sideways for a few steps before dropping down to the four-footed stance. He hits or breaks anything in his path, which makes this a dangerous moment. Schaller once saw a juvenile picked up by a running male and thrown down a slope. The other gorillas seem to know what to expect when a silver-back starts to display, and hurriedly get out of the way.

This may sound like the essence of violence, but the scientist finds interesting comparisons with human behavior. Gorillas, he says, are introverts, not volatile and excitable like the chimpanzees. They conceal their emotions. This display is a valve for letting off steam. And he reminds us of the behavior of a human audience at a baseball game, where people stand up, shout in unison, and often throw bottles and other things onto the field.

In addition to braving the exaggerated dangers of gorillaland without a gun, Schaller also opposed the depredations of poachers and encroachers who tried to overrun the park at the time of Congo independence. The white administrators of the park fled in fear of revolutionary violence. But the new young black administrator soon arrived and put his authority behind Schaller's protests. The park was saved, and the gorillas were assured a safe home, for a time at least. The new Congo government fortunately understands the need for protecting this closest relative of mankind.

Bibliography

Allen, Glover Morrill, *Bats,* Dover Publications, Inc. New York, 1962

Babcock, Harold L., *Turtles of the Northeastern United States,* Dover Publications, Inc. New York, 1971

Barbour, Roger W. and Davis, Wayne H., *Bats of America,* University of Kentucky Press, Lexington, Ky., 1969

Beebe, B. F., *American Lions and Cats,* David McKay Company, Inc., New York, 1963

Bent, Arthur Cleveland, "Life Histories of North American Birds of Prey," Part I, *U.S. National Museum,* Bulletin #167

Burton, R. W., "The Indian Wild Dog," *Journal of The Bombay Natural History Society,* Vol. 41

Caras, Roger A., *Dangerous to Man,* Chilton Book Company, Philadelphia and New York, 1964

Carr, Archie, *Handbook of Turtles of the United States, Canada and Baja, California,* Cornell University Press, Ithaca, N.Y., 1952

Cousteau, Jacques-Yves, "Housekeeper of the Deep," *International Wildlife,* March–April, 1973

———— and Philippe Diole, "Killer Whales Have Fearsome Teeth," *Smithsonian Magazine*

Davids, Richard C., "Pigs, Those True-Blue Americans," *Science Digest,* September, 1969

Deas, Walter, "Venomous Octopus," *Sea Frontiers,* Vol. 16, #6

Durrell, Gerald, *Encounters with Animals,* Avon Book Division, New York, 1970

Fabbri, Roberto, "Manta Pup," *Sea Frontiers,* Vol. 17, #6, November–December, 1971

Green, Otis, "Love Call of a Porcupine," *Nature Magazine,* January, 1956

Griffin, Edward I., "Making Friends With A Killer Whale," *National Geographic,* March, 1966

Hammer, Donald A., "The Durable Snapping Turtle," *Natural History,* June, 1971

Harvey, Paul W., Jr., "Oregon State Questions Federal Predator Program," *Defenders of Wildlife News,* Spring, 1971

Hass, Hans, *Manta,* Rand McNally & Company, Chicago, 1953

Holdsworth, John B., "Peccaries," *National Wildlife,* February, 1969

Hornocker, Maurice G., "Stalking the Mountain Lion To Save Him," *National Geographic,* November, 1969

Krott, Peter, *Tupu-Tupu-Tupu,* Hutchinson & Co., Ltd., London, 1958

Kruuk, Hans, "A New View of the Hyena," *New Scientist,* Vol. 30, #502, 1966

———— "Hyenas, The Hunters Nobody Knows," *National Geographic,* July, 1968

LaBastille, Anne, "Vampire: Black Sheep of the Bat Family," *International Wildlife,* March–April, 1973

Lane, Frank W., *Kingdom of The Octopus,* Pyramid Books, New York, 1962

Lawrence, H. Lea, "Wild Boar of The Appalachians," *Natural History,* October, 1969

Middleton, A., "The Indian Wild Dog," *Journal of the Bombay Natural History Society,* Vol. 50

Morris, Desmond, *The Mammals,* Harper & Row, Publishers, Inc., New York, 1965

Mowery, William Byron, *Swift in the Night,* Coward-McCann Inc., New York, 1956

Murphy, Robert, *The Mountain Lion,* E. P. Dutton & Co., Inc., New York, 1969

Murray, Justin, "Mutiny on the Bounty System," *Defenders of Wildlife News,* March, 1972

Owings, Margaret, "The Mountain Lion in California," *Defenders of Wildlife News,* Spring, 1971

Peacock, E. H., "A Note on the Malayan Wild Dog," *Journal of the Bombay Natural History Society,* Vol. 33

Peterson, Russell, *Silently, By Night,* McGraw-Hill Book Company, New York, 1964

Poling, James, "Creature of Air and Darkness," *Marvels and Mysteries of Our Animal World,* Reader's Digest Assn., Pleasantville, N.Y., 1964

Reynolds, Vernon, *The Apes,* E. P. Dutton & Co., New York, 1967

Robey, W. F., Jr., "Puma," *Defenders of Wildlife News,* March, 1972

Rood, Ronald, *Animals Nobody Loves,* Stephen Green Press, Brattleboro, Vt., 1971

———— *How Do You Spank A Porcupine?,* Trident Press, New York, 1969

———— *Wild Brother,* Pocket Books, New York, 1971

Rutter, Russell J. and Pimlott, Douglas H., *The World of the Wolf,* J. B. Lippincott Company, Philadelphia and New York, 1968

Schaller, George B., "A Naturalist in South Asia," *New York Zoological Society Report,* Spring, 1971

—— *The Year of the Gorilla,* The University of Chicago Press, 1964

Scheffer, Victor B., "The Cliché of The Killer," *Natural History,* October, 1970

Spencer, Donald A., "Porcupines, Rambling Pincushions," *National Geographic,* August, 1950

Terres, John K., "Adventures with Vultures," *Audubon Magazine,* January, 1968

Thomas, Bill, "The Buzzards of Hinckley," *National Wildlife,* February, 1969

Van Lawick-Goodall, Hugo and Jane, *Innocent Killers,* Houghton Mifflin Company, Boston, 1971

Voss, Gilbert L., "Shy Monster, The Octopus," *National Geographic,* December, 1971

Walker, Ernest P., *Mammals of The World,* The Johns Hopkins Press, Baltimore, 1968

Weddle, Ferris, "Following The Wolverine's Trails," *Defenders of Wildlife News,* Spring, 1971

—— "Secrets of The Mighty Cougar," *National Wildlife,* October–November, 1970

Winterbotham, Joyce C., "A Wild Dog Incident," *Journal of the Bombay Natural History Society,* Vol. 50

Zeuner, F. E., *A History of Domesticated Animals,* Harper & Row, Publishers, Inc., New York, 1963

Index